College 101

Campus Life for Christians

CONCORDIA PUBLISHING HOUSE · SAINT LOUIS

Copyright © 2010 Concordia Publishing House
3558 S. Jefferson Ave., St. Louis, MO 63118-3968
1-800-325-3040 • www.cph.org

Illustrations by Jon Cannell.

This publication may be available in braille, in large print, or on cassette tape for the visually impaired. Please allow 8 to 12 weeks for delivery. Write to Lutheran Blind Mission, 7550 Watson Rd., St. Louis, MO 63119-4409; call toll-free 1-888-215-2455; or visit the Web site: www.blindmission.org.

Manufactured in the United States of America

Library of Congress Cataloging-in-Publication Data

College 101 : campus life for Christians
      p. cm.
  ISBN 978-0-7586-1906-8
  1. Christian college students—Religious life. 2. College student orientation. I. Title.

  BV4531.3.C57 2010
  248.8'34—dc22

                                                    2009043389

1 2 3 4 5 6 7 8 9 10   19 18 17 16 15 14 13 12 11 10

Our thanks to…

The awesome student authors:

Amanda Bach—Eastern Illinois University

Rachel Fickenscher—Indiana University

Lauren Fontaine—Florida State University

Colleen Kitka—Eastern Illinois University

Eric Mennel—Florida State University

Kelsey Paulsen—Concordia University, Irvine

Wesley Smith—Indiana University

Jessica Ulrich—Kansas State University

Ann Voss—Eastern Illinois University

Amber White—Maryville University

and our consultants:

Gregory Witto, Immanuel Lutheran Church, Charleston, IL & LCMS Campus Ministry for Eastern Illinois University

Pastor Marty Marks, Immanuel Lutheran Church, DeKalb, IL & LCMS Campus Ministry for Northern Illinois University

Table of Contents

introduction

Welcome to **College 101**. Perhaps you just graduated from high school or are preparing to graduate soon. Maybe you've already spent some time on a college campus. Whatever your situation, we're glad you decided to check out this resource.

College 101: Campus Life for Christians was written with you in mind. In each chapter, our student authors share their real-life campus experiences. The author panel includes students from major universities, small private colleges, and everything in between. You'll learn from their successes as well as their mistakes. Most important, you'll hear firsthand what it means to be a Christian student on campus today.

Before You Go

Graduation celebrations are winding down, so now you look forward to a summer job and earning some cash before you take your next step toward freedom. Just a couple of years ago, I was in those same shoes, excited and scared about the next few years. I'm sure you're thinking that life is becoming more and more complicated every day as you approach your first day of college classes. You have high hopes for what the next few years have to offer, or perhaps you have many worries and reservations about the years to come. Before you even leave home, you face difficult decisions that will shape your college experience. What should you do to prepare? What roommate situation works best for you? What clothes do you take? What high school memories do you pack away as you fit your life into cardboard boxes? What do your parents expect of you in this new chapter of your life?

The good news is that you are not alone. All high school seniors face certain fears and questions as they prepare for independent adulthood. For many, this means taking the first step toward college or university. Don't panic. Take a deep breath and remember that your Savior will always be with you as He walks right beside you (Deuteronomy 31:6; Psalm 23).

We will answer some of your questions to help form a clearer vision about what to expect in the months and years ahead. While I may not know you personally, perhaps you can learn from my experiences, both good and bad, as you make informed decisions before heading off to campus.

||||||||||||||||||||||||||

My parents are supportive, but I don't know what they expect.

Everyone has different reasons for going to college. For some, the decision is fueled by parental expectations. For others, it is based on individual dreams. Still others view their college choice as a combination of the two. Figuring out your true motives behind your college choice may be the most challenging thing you do before you head off to school. Hopefully, you are following your personal dream. In any case, you should talk to your parents to see what they expect from your college choices.

Take the time to sit down with your parents before you head off to school to see what they expect from you so you do not end up disappointing them unintentionally. A few topics you should include in your conversation are alcohol and drug use, grades, relationships, finances, and church attendance. These topics will be addressed in later chapters in this book.

I chose my roommate. Now what do I expect?

Choosing your roommate situation will be one of the first major decisions you have to make before you head off to school. The results of this decision affect your life on campus in a major way. With most schools, you have two options for choosing your roommate: room with someone you already know or take your chances with a open assignment.

If you choose to room with someone you already know, consider the following: How well do you know your future roommate? Does your future roommate share your Christian faith?

There are three possible answers to the first question: you know your future roommate very well; you know the individual a little bit; or he or she is an acquaintance. Knowing the depth of your relationship with this person will help you make an educated decision.

So what does it mean to know a person very well? In most cases, it means you consider this person your best friend, almost as if you are a brother or sister to the person. You share everything, and you spend a great deal of time together.

If you classify your relationship with your potential roommate as very close, rooming together may still not be the best choice. I've personally witnessed two potential outcomes for best friends who room together. The first is that you will end up becoming even closer. I have numerous friends who ended up strengthening their relationship by rooming with their best friend. But another possible outcome of choosing to room with your best friend is that you end up stressing your relationship to the point of causing a rift between the two of you. Unfortunately, in the cases I've seen, this latter scenario is the more likely of the two. I know numerous cases where best friends have roomed together but before the end of the first semester, they have changed roommates.

The second option, in my opinion, is the best choice—rooming with someone you know a little bit. Because you do not have as great an expectation for how the person will act as a roommate, you have the opportunity to get to know your roommate better and you can grow in your friendship. Two of my really close friends just barely knew each other in high school. They became best friends their freshman year of college, and they had no problem adjusting to each other. My freshman roommate was someone I knew in high school, but whom I did not know well. The living situation took some time for my roommate and me to get used to, but we eventually adjusted and became good friends.

Being acquaintances is the final possible type of relationship you can have with your chosen roommate. This I would describe as almost a blind date. Perhaps someone refers another person to you that he or she thinks would be a good roommate for you. This is close to potluck, but you are matched up by a person who knows you well. This, I guess, takes the luck out of potluck. Most pairings like this turn out well because the referral allows you to be paired with someone who has similar beliefs or morals.

The other major thing I would suggest you consider in selecting a roommate is answering the question "Does he/she share my Christian faith?" The answer to this question will allow you to choose a roommate that you can know how to live with. If your roommate is a Christian, expect someone who will help keep you accountable to your beliefs. My first roommate was a Christian. At times, he would wake me up to talk about the Bible or a statement he heard in a study group. While this may not be a typical course of action for a Christian roommate to take, you can expect someone like that to make sure you stay true to your faith.

If your roommate is not a Christian, you can expect a lot of exposure to situations you may have never even thought of. My second roommate is not a Christian, and this allowed me an opportunity to witness how my faith affects the things I do in my life. He has always been open to talking about my beliefs, and he has voiced his beliefs. But until I met him, I did not know such beliefs even existed in our world. As a Christian with a non-Christian roommate, be prepared for potential conflicts in values. Also watch out for the temptation to avoid talking about worship or other faith-sustaining practices. It is especially important to make sure that you surround yourself with fellow believers in a group Bible study or campus ministry so you have opportunities to meet with others who share your faith.

||||||||||||||||||||||||||||

I do not want to know my roommate. What can I expect in choosing to live with a stranger?

Okay, so you have decided that you do not know anyone attending your college of choice who would work well as a roommate. What can you expect? First, I want to commend your courage. Don't worry—most of these situations work out well. From my experience, there are two potential outcomes from a potluck roommate assignment: you will gain a new best friend or you will become enemies.

Great! Okay. So now you're thinking, I can become best friends with my new roommate. What a great attitude to have! More times than not, I have seen this housing situation have positive results. You come in without any notions about what your roommate will act like, so you tend to be more open toward the person and his or her actions. This helps you develop a relationship with your new roommate that will take time to develop. Many of my friends did not know each other before they roomed together. Now they are returning as roommates for the second or third year.

Okay. So I've scared you, and you're thinking, I'm afraid my roommate will be intolerable. In some cases, this is a legitimate fear. Be prepared to handle each situation with class, and let Christ shine through you. Start out by talking to your roommate. Develop a set of guidelines to help avoid future misunderstandings.

||||||||||||||||||||||||||||||

Learn about your roommate.

Now it's time to get down to the nitty-gritty. Contact your roommate before move-in to discuss many issues. If you're rooming with someone you already know, this is easy. If you don't already know your future roommate, you may not know how to contact the person. Many universities provide either a phone number or e-mail of your future roommate. If they do not, you can check Facebook, MySpace, or other social networking sites to see if you can find your future roommate and discuss the upcoming school year.

When you contact your roommate, there are two topics I suggest you discuss. You should talk about guidelines and who is bringing shared items such as a refrigerator or television. Guidelines are fairly simple; they tell you what to expect of your new roommate and of yourself. This gives you a chance to start adjusting early so you can meet the guidelines you are setting for yourselves. Roommate guidelines could include alarm-clock issues, expected study hours, and so forth. Basically, you have to mesh your two lifestyles for the next school year. For shared supplies, you need to figure out who is bringing what. My past two roommates brought refrigerators, but I supplied the microwave. Usually, you need only one refrigerator and one microwave in your room. Other things you might want to talk about bringing are televisions, game systems, and movies.

Okay, I get it. Now what do I bring?

By now you are either getting very excited or slightly panicked. Hopefully, it's more excited, but you are still wondering what is left to cover. In the past few years, I have developed a set of guidelines for myself that I would like to share with you in order to keep your moving list to a minimum. Each year I have cut the number of items I bring with me to school because I realize I do not end up needing everything I bring. Here is the quick reference to my set of guidelines:

- Golden Rule

- Rule of Fourteen

- Rule of Movies

- Time-Passer Rule

- Rule of Computers

Now I've probably confused you with my little rule names, but I created these names to help you remember the important stuff.

Golden Rule

The Golden Rule is simply to remember your Bible. Consider getting a new Bible to use at school, one that you can use as a study companion as you grow in Christ. Bibles such as *The Lutheran Study Bible* will help you gain insight to Scripture through the study notes and background information. You may not always be near a pastor or know how to find a specific reference or Bible passage, so having a Bible with easy-to-use notes and a good concordance is important. Also, having your Bible in your room offers a witness opportunity. I don't expect you to shove your Bible in everyone's face. Simply leave it out on your desk for others to see. Its mere presence can be a conversation starter as well as your opportunity to share your faith without forcing your beliefs on a friend or acquaintance. One other positive result of bringing your Bible is that you can have it as a study companion if you are unable to attend a Bible study regularly.

Rule of Fourteen

The Rule of Fourteen is simple. I suggest that you bring fourteen days' worth of clothes with you to school. Admittedly, this rule is easier for me as a guy. For an average person, this would include fourteen sets of clothes (underwear, socks, shirts, pants). Athletes who work out or run each day will probably need a few more outfits. The Rule of Fourteen does not take into account church or "dressy" clothes, only those for daily wear. The reason for fourteen sets of clothes is to force you to do your laundry every two weeks. This keeps your room from smelling and/or your clothes to begin rotting away. Perhaps you think "rotting" is a bit of an exaggeration, but my freshman year, my roommate and I did not do laundry until the end of the first month. You could smell our room through the closed door. We had brought way too many clothes, so the laundry just piled up. This past year, I readjusted my clothing plan, which forced me to do laundry every two weeks. This kept my room from smelling nasty and kept my dorm mates happy.

Rule of Movies

The Rule of Movies is fairly simple. I suggest you pick just five to ten of your favorite movies to bring to college. You really don't need your entire 100+ movie collection with you at school. If you need a movie, you can pick it up from the library or rent it. For the most part, you will have time to watch only your favorite movies. I made the mistake of bringing my entire movie (and game) collection my freshman year. This took up a huge amount of the very limited space in the van (for the trip to school) and then in my room.

Time-Passer Rule

I recommend bringing the equipment for one or two activities that you love to do in your free time. Bringing these items helps you escape from the stressful situations you are bound to experience while at college. I bring my running shoes. My friends know when I am stressed because they see me walking down the hall in running shorts and a T-shirt, ready to go on a run.

Your time-passer equipment also allows you to have a short break between study sessions. I have been encouraged by many people to take a fifteen-minute break between two-hour study sessions. This break helps me retain more of what I am studying. During that break, I pick up my guitar and play. Now I'm sure some of my friends consider my guitar breaks a plague, but they help me relax before I go back to straining my brain.

Rule of Computers

The final rule is the Rule of Computers. Be sure to bring one computer. Many people ask, "Should I bring a laptop or a desktop?" I would recommend a laptop. Most professors on my campus do not allow laptop computers in their classroom because they find computers distract students as they are trying to teach. Other universities may require students to use computers in the classroom. Check with upper-class students at your university to discover the trend at your school.

Though most of your work will be done in your dorm room, I recommend a laptop so that you have the flexibility to work on your homework and papers in other places. Also, I recommend bringing a printer. Numerous times I went to the printing center in my dorm and found that it was locked. Yes, it was supposed to be open twenty-four hours a day, but it was closed when I needed it. One of my friends went to print off a midterm paper thirty minutes before it was due, but the printer was jammed. He had to run to the library to print his paper just a few minutes before it was due. You do not want to experience this disaster, so having your own printer as a backup is a good idea.

There are some items I would recommend that you avoid bringing to school. Leave your video game system at home. These games can be a huge distraction when your primary task at school is to study. I would also avoid bringing furniture. Most dorms provide you with all the necessities. Adding furniture to a room that is already pretty full will clutter your space. It seems I always had some type of chair that just got in the way of the flow of the room, and my room seemed to shrink very quickly. Friends who stopped by commented that their room was much bigger, even though the floor plans were identical.

Finally, you have all your stuff ready to go, but not everything will fit into your parents' car. You've followed my advice, but now you're stuck and you don't know what to cut. I would recommend first cutting your distractions. You are not at school to learn to play video games or guitar (unless, of course, you're a music major).

|||||||||||||||||||||||||||||

I think I'm ready. Anything else?

So we've talked about possible roommate situations, what to bring and what not to bring, and what to talk to your parents about. You may be thinking there's nothing else to really think about before you head off to college. However, there is one last thing you need to think about before you go: how to bring Christ along to college.

I realize it's not literally possible for you to leave Christ behind, because since He promises to be with us wherever we go: "I am with you always, to the end of the age" (Matthew 28:20). However, you will face many people who are not Christians. You may or may not know how to handle each situation that you face. If you prepare for your college experience with Christ, you will be equipped to adjust and handle these situations much more easily than had you not prepared. Consider this three-part plan as you get ready for your life on campus:

Dig into the Scriptures

This summer, get to know your Bible better than ever. Even if it has been a while since you seriously read the Scriptures, take the time to read God's Word, even just fifteen minutes a day. If you want an organized plan for reading through the Scriptures, check out the resources available from your local congregation or **www.cph.org/luth eranbible**.

Attend or Host a Summer Bible Study

Consider being part of a summer Bible study group. You might ask your pastor or someone else at you church to conduct a special Bible study group for students just entering or already attending various universities. Most students return home during the summer months to work or visit families. This offers a perfect opportunity for you to get acquainted with students already in college as you grow in your understanding of God's Word.

Identify Your Campus Church Home

Many colleges and universities host special orientation sessions during the summer months. Use this time to check out the campus ministry you plan to attend. In some cases, this may be a campus chapel affiliated with your church body. In other cases, it may be a local church that welcomes students to be part of their congregation during the school year. If you have questions, your home pastor can help you locate and connect with a church home while at school.

||||||||||||||||||||||||||||

But Wait! There's More!

Did you really think you were done? We're just getting started! There are many things to think about as you head off to college. Keep reading to hear more advice from our panel of college authors.

 W.S.

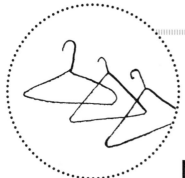

Move-In Mania

The bags were all packed, and the car was loaded. Jamie watched as her two siblings, Jacob and Alicia, pulled out of the driveway on their way to high school. Tears welled up in her eyes. By the time they came home again this afternoon, she'd be gone. Today was the day! Today was the start of something new, something different, something exciting. Today was the day when she would be saying good-bye to her past life and hello to the great unknown. Today was the day when Jamie would make the long trek with her mom and dad to that place called "college."

College! Jamie could not believe it was finally time. All her life, she had been a little nervous of the day when she would have to leave her family, her friends, and everything she held dear in order to go to a place where she would have to live with a total stranger and eat meals made by someone besides her mom. Although everyone had told her that college would be the time of her life, Jamie was not so sure.

On the one hand, she was frightened that she would not be able to make friends and that her classes would be ten times harder than the classes she had taken in high school. On the other hand, she kept telling herself that maybe everyone was right. Maybe college would be the time of her life. Maybe her roommate would become her best friend and her freedom from her parents would allow her to open up more and find out for herself who she was as a person. Maybe she would become passionate about her major and excited to find out what her future would bring. Perhaps, even, she would meet a cute boy whom she would someday call her husband. Who knew? Yes, Jamie thought to herself, she could learn to like this thing called college.

"Are you all ready?" her father asked. Jamie snapped out of her daydream and realized this was the moment. She would now have to squeeze into the packed car and leave her house for what seemed like forever. After saying a quick prayer asking the Lord to give her strength and guidance during this next chapter of her life, Jamie shut the car door, and they were off.

Every student leaving home for the start of his or her freshman year of college has gone through a day more or less like Jamie's. Saying good-bye to brothers and sisters, driving with mom and dad to school, unpacking the car, meeting the new roommate, saying good-bye to mom and dad. It can all seem rather intimidating. A lot of good-byes, a lot of encounters with the unknown. As much as a person would try to prepare, there was no way of knowing exactly what to expect. Although there is no way to put into words what a soon-to-be freshman would be feeling on that first day of college, this chapter will give a taste of what it would be like. The sights, the sounds, the tears, and the laughter of "move-in mania."

Mania. That is exactly what it is—mania. Some describe move-in day as stressful, hectic, and chaotic. Others say that it is exciting, thrilling, and maybe even tons of fun. However one describes it, everyone would agree that relaxing is not in the mix. No matter what school a person decides to attend, on move-in day there is no avoiding the large crowds, long lines, and anxious students and parents. As mentioned earlier, many find this day exciting. With the right attitude going into this day, it can be fun for everyone. It's fun to think that so many people could have the same goal and purpose at the same time and place . . . finding a way to make themselves or their children comfortable in their new home away from home.

During the drive to college, the closer one gets to the destination, the more jam-packed cars are seen on the highway, filled with televisions, fridges, clothes on hangers, and bedspreads. University decals or bumper stickers adorn these same cars with phrases such as "Go Hoosiers" and "Proud Trojan Parent." Traffic will probably be horrendous because all these cars are going to the same place, but that's part of the fun! The students and parents in these cars have similar fears and expectations racing through their heads. No one is alone! To avoid some added stress, however, leave home earlier than planned and expect heavy traffic. This way, you and your family can really enjoy their last hours together without becoming too stressed.

Once the family van pulls into the turn-around in front of the student's new dorm, the mania continues. Now all those cars you saw on the highway (well, maybe not exactly *all* of them) seem to be lined up waiting to disgorge their contents. As fathers unload everything from the back, mothers stake out an area on the pavement to place everything, and children get into the long line to receive dorm keys, meal cards, and so forth. Then the students help their parents move all of their belongings into the empty room they now call home.

At this point, one of three situations might occur:

- Situation A: Student's new roommate has not yet arrived; therefore, the student has the prerogative to start thinking about where items such as the television, microwave, and refrigerator should be placed.

- Situation B: Roommate has already come and then gone out, leaving behind somewhat of a setup of where everything should go.

- Situation C: Roommate confrontation.

Situation C—the most feared situation of them all by many students. Up until this moment, every soon-to-be freshman has worried about the new roommate. What will he be like? Will she like me? What will we talk about? I hope we don't have one of those awkward relationships where neither person talks. All of these thoughts have at one time or another passed through every college student's mind, and as the student finds his roommate in his new room, he realizes that now is the time he must be friendly, make a good first impression, and branch out. It's human nature to be a little shy around strangers. It's easy enough to talk only to those people one has known all his life, but at this point, hiding behind one's friends is no longer possible.

So how should meeting the roommate be handled? As cheesy as it sounds, a hug or handshake (whatever seems more comfortable) really can make the difference between starting a lasting friendship and starting a long, awkward semester. Good eye contact is also important. These gestures let one's new roommate know right away that he is excited to meet him and that friendship is a realistic option. Also, hopefully by now, the students have been in contact by Facebook or the phone, and they know a little bit about the other person. Hobbies, pets, siblings—these simple topics make for good introductory conversation. On top of this, both students will soon begin moving all of their stuff in from their cars, so discussing where furniture items should be placed is an easy way to break the ice.

After an hour or so, the room is packed with two people's belongings. Some are put away; some are still sitting in the middle of the floor. All this hard work calls for a bit of a celebration! It's lunchtime, and since the parents won't be seeing their child for quite a long time, it's likely the idea of going out to a nice restaurant could come up. Some families decide to invite the roommate's family along so they can get to know one another better. Other families like to fully savor their last moments together and decide to eat alone. Either way, good food is enjoyed by all!

While still out and about, someone will remember items needed for the new room, so a trip to Target or Walmart is in order. What surprises most people is how many other families had the exact same idea. In big college towns, move-in day might be the busiest day of the year for these stores, maybe even busier than the day after Thanksgiving! How these stores prepare for the college rush is incredible. At the ends of all the aisles, stores strategically place tons of fridges, televisions, futons—all of the hot items for a college dorm room. And, boy, do these items go fast! Some students come in just for the odds and ends they forgot to bring along, while others are there to begin their college shopping (one way to avoid running out of room in the family van). Whatever the shoppers' motives, these stores are certainly the places to be!

With more stuff purchased and the movers fed, it is about time for a tradition that in one shape or form is present at almost all colleges—Freshman Induction. Ah, yes! All hail to our fair school, and welcome, freshmen, to the greatest years of your lives. At Indiana University, words such as "Gloriana" and "Frangipana" (words made up to rhyme with Indiana) are heard for the first time as parents and students sing the school's Alma Mater. The president of the university delivers his first speech of the year, and students are told to do their best to not get lost in the crowd. For many parents, this is the time when reality sets in. In a matter of hours, their child will be alone in a place where she must make her own choices; choices such as actually going to class and choosing to avoid taking part in illegal activities. The main part of a parent's job is complete, and it is now up to the child to decide how life plays out.

At the conclusion of the ceremony, many colleges invite the new students and parents to a dinner or picnic in celebration of the start of the new school year. People are invited to mingle with fellow students and even professors in an attempt to make incoming students feel more comfortable in their new surroundings. At the conclusion of this picnic, parents are asked to say good-bye to their loved ones. Their kids are all grown up, and it's finally time to let them go. Some depart with tears in their eyes. Others leave with smiles on their faces and pride in their hearts for their child's success so far in life. It's quite a sentimental time, handled by everyone in his or her own way.

Now that the parents have gone back to their respective homes, it seems as if move-in day has already lasted forever. Alas, it is only 6:00 p.m., and the evening has just begun. The next event of the day is the first floor meeting of the year. At this meeting, new students are introduced to others who will be living on their dorm floor for the year. The floor's RA (residential assistant) runs the meeting by introducing herself (or himself), explaining the general rules of dorm life, and making everyone feel as comfortable as possible. An icebreaker game might be played in order for everyone to get more acquainted. As annoying as these games sometimes seem, they're great because they usually result in some sort of silly episode that people laugh together about during the rest of the week. People's personalities shine through as well, so everyone gets a good feeling about what the coming year might bring and an idea about who would be fun to hang out with.

All right, now here comes the good part! With everyone moved in, the rules laid out, and the logistics taken care of, the fun begins! Move-in day is the start of a half-week-or-so-long celebration. For some, Welcome Week, a time of socializing, free food, and no school, is the best time of the year. Basically, students get to experience college life without having to worry about *silly* stuff like homework, tests, and grades. Seriously, though, as important as your education is, what makes college so special and "the time of one's life" are the friends you meet and the memories you make together. Classes shouldn't be blown off once they start, but there's something to be said about keeping a healthy balance between work and play. It'll be no fun twenty years down the line to look back and regret not taking advantage of all the great opportunities college had to offer. Anyway, Welcome Week is the beginning of this social side of college. It's the first time for many students to be so far away from home, and universities make sure that this week is a blast for everyone.

At some universities, each dorm sponsors evening activities the first night that include a free meal and maybe even free T-shirts. Grilled burgers and hot dogs could be the fare at one dorm, while carnival treats such as cotton candy, ice cream, and snow cones could be present at the next. Most students usually stay at their dorm's party, socializing with their fellow residents, but a select few decide to take full advantage of the situation by party hopping from one dorm to the next. Why not? It's totally free and totally legit. If you pay close enough attention to flyers and information written in chalk on the sidewalks, you can probably find free food at three or more events per day of Welcome Week. Some students look back and realize they did not have to spend a single meal point in the dorm cafeterias before classes started because of all the events they attended!

While you're having all this fun, it's important to realize there will be two very different types of parties going on during Welcome Week. The ones mentioned earlier are all sponsored by college organizations such as dorms, sports intramural groups, or the honors college. These parties allow people to get to know other students interested in similar activities as they in a fun, low-key sort of way.

But this type of party is not the only one offered during Welcome Week at many universities. Many fraternities and sororities, along with upperclassmen living off campus, will host welcome-back socials where students of all ages can mingle. Unfortunately, these parties tend to focus on drinking and "partying hard." To some new freshmen, this seems like the only or easiest way to make friends. Some people think that they will act "cooler" or "more outgoing" when they are drunk, so going to frat parties is a no-brainer when trying to meet new people. Sadly, because of this, Welcome Week is also the time when many young students get into trouble with the law, or worse. Students need to be warned that if they put themselves into illegal, dangerous situations, good probably won't result. It's easy enough for an upperclassman to see a lonely freshman taking a walk by herself and ask her if she would like to join him at the "happenin'" party down the road. Thinking this is the only way to make friends, the girl might accept the guy's offer and hop into his car. Making wise decisions is important in college, and if a student starts partying even before classes start, it's quite likely that this will become his main source of entertainment for the rest of college. To read more about frat parties and other temptations, take a look at chapter 5.

So, how should a new student make friends? Well, getting to know your roommate is a good place to start. As soon as you two are somewhat comfortable with each other, you can go to different on-campus events to meet other students. It's much easier to approach someone new if a freshman knows his roommate will help him get through the introductory conversations. Getting to know others living on your dorm floor is also very important. These floormates are the ones you will see and live with all year long, so it's good to make friends. Floor dinners . . . now there's an idea! Some floors make it a point to eat together at least once a week, while others eat together even more frequently. It's a good bonding experience that causes people to grow close very quickly. Yes, the first couple of meals will be pretty awkward. Some people try to start up a conversation by asking others about their interests, while others are really shy and just sit there. But, hey! How else are you supposed to get to know one another? That's how this kind of thing works! As the days and weeks progress, the freshman floor becomes a close-knit group of friends who will barely even remember those awkward first conversations.

All right, so the roommates and the floormates are all friends. How do you go about making other friends? It's hard to believe until you actually go to college, but a certain phenomenon occurs there that is found nowhere else. Strangers actually go out of their way to talk to one another! As a college freshman, it is quite likely that most of your high school friends will not be joining you at the same college, so it is necessary to make new ones. Most new students feel like they are in the same situation—alone in a new place where they must create a new life for themselves, including new friends. Start out by just saying hi or even just smiling. Imagine that! A simple hello and a few friendly statements can turn two complete strangers into lifelong friends! So freshmen shouldn't be shy. Putting your best foot forward and introducing yourself can be easier than it might seem! It's not like high school, where many of the kids have been friends since grade school, and a transfer student from the local parochial school might have a hard time fitting in. In college, everyone's new, everyone's nervous, and everyone's in need of friends. Just being friendly is the way to go!

One trap some students fall into is hanging out with the few high school friends they know at college throughout Welcome Week. Townies (students who are from the same city as their college) seem to fall into this trap even more easily since some of their younger friends might still be in town finishing high school. Hanging out with old friends is not in itself a bad thing, but in the long run, you might regret it. After classes start, people seem to prefer hanging out with the people they met during this first week. If you spend all your time with high school friends, it's likely that making other friends later on will seem difficult, if not impossible. For this reason, it is crucial that everyone does his best to branch out, be friendly, and meet someone new.

One more crucial task remains before classes start—buying textbooks. Some students preorder their books through Web sites such as Amazon.com, while others wait to go to the college bookstore at the end of Welcome Week. As you might guess, the lines to purchase these books are horrible! During the busiest days right before classes begin, bookstore lines can take an hour or longer to get through! For this reason (as well as the fact that online retailers generally offer better prices), online purchasing is a good way to go. If shopping the college bookstore route is your method of choice, find an upperclassman willing to show you the ropes. The bookstores aren't that confusing once you get the hang of them, but it is nice to have a helping hand the first time around. During your college years, you will spend hundreds (probably thousands) of dollars on textbooks. Look for bookstore rewards programs. If there's a prize for spending so much money in one place, why not take advantage?

After a fun, exciting week filled with new surprises, new people, and the occasional phone call home, Sunday night eventually rolls around. Just like when you first left your parents and headed off to kindergarten, you will find this to be one of the few times in life when the first day of school is super thrilling and super nerve-racking all at the same time. Not knowing what to expect, the average freshman decides to pack his backpack before he heads to bed, in fear that he might leave something behind the next day. Some students (especially girls) even lay out their clothes for the next day, picking out the outfit sure to receive a compliment. As cheesy as "dress to impress" sounds, people find that if they look their best, they also feel their best. The better a person feels, the more confident he or she will be, and the more confident he or she is, the more likely it is that others will want to be friends and know more about him or her. Getting one awesome back-to-school outfit to wear the first day of class might be nice to look into. It's an easy way to help your first day be as good as it can be.

Finally, one last tip, in preparation for the first day of classes—get some sleep! While I'm not trying to sound like your mother, sleep is important, and if a freshman is planning on making a good impression in class, being wide awake that first day is very important. It's just one more way to increase confidence and rock that first day of school!

Phew! What a week this has been! And to think how just a few days ago everyone was just like Jamie, nervous that he or she would hate college and never make friends! My, how it has changed! Looking back, though, how did it all happen? How is it possible that it worked out so wonderfully? Remember that simple prayer Jamie prayed before leaving in her family's van? "Lord, give me strength and guidance during this next chapter in my life." Her prayer was not in vain. Nobody's prayer to the Lord Jesus Christ is ever in vain. God promises to hear all our prayers and answer them in the best way, in His timing. Don't ever forget what He so graciously invites us to do: "Humble yourselves, therefore, under the mighty hand of God so that at the proper time He may exalt you, casting all your anxieties on Him, because He cares for you" (1 Peter 5:6–7). That's right. He cares for and loves everyone in this world and wishes to be with them during those rough, scary times, along with all the other times of their lives.

So what is there to worry about? As God promised Joshua in the Old Testament, "Be strong and courageous. Do not be frightened, and do not be dismayed, for the Lord your God is with you wherever you go" (Joshua 1:9). God just as sincerely promises to be with all people during life's journey. This includes those first terrifying days of college, which many find to be the most awesome days of their lives so far. As crazy as move-in mania can be, it sure is great knowing that Christians have a God who promises all of this and so much more!

 R.F.

three

Dorm Away from Home

Welcome to your new home! We realize you have lots of reading to do, so if you don't have time for the whole chapter, here's a top-ten list.

1. Lock your door at night. (Keep reading to find out why.)

2. Get out and socialize.

3. Be respectful and considerate to everyone and everything.

4. Keep your keys and school ID on you at all times.

5. Learn how to do laundry before you leave home.

6. Elevators will break; get used to the stairs.

7. Wear shower shoes—flip-flops get the job done.

8. Naps are your friend.

9. Don't forget your alarm clock or your Bible! (More than one way to wake up.)

10. Remember to give your dorm address to friends and family because getting mail is rare and can be the highlight of your day!

||||||||||||||||||||||||||

Dorm Types

You've made the big decision of where to go to school. The next step is choosing where to live. Most schools offer a variety of housing options, so these decisions depend on your personal preferences. Different dorm types include coed versus same gender and single, double, or even triple rooms.

Co-ed dorms have males and females all living in the same building. This could mean each floor is divided by gender, with a floor of males and then a floor of females alternating throughout the building. There are also buildings that have co-ed floors. Floors could be divided into wings or in half in order to separate males and females. Rarely do you find males and females randomly dispersed throughout the floor.

For obvious reasons, most parents prefer single-gender dorms, meaning every floor of the building is either all females or all males. Most single-gender dorms also have restricted visiting hours and related rules when it comes to escorting your guest around the floor. It is important to take into consideration all positives and negatives of either living arrangement. Parents may have their own opinions that might be more heavily weighted because they are usually the ones paying for college (and we are all grateful for that).

Roommates can either make or break your freshman dorm experience. Room options include living by yourself (singles are rarely offered to freshmen), with one other roommate (double), or even living with two or more roommates (triple, quad, etc.). Living by yourself might sound like it will be so much fun and easier, but when you get the chance to live with someone else, you learn about yourself as a person, learn how to live with someone who may be different than you, and begin a possible lifelong friendship. It has been said that college is where you meet the people who could become your friends for life.

The norm for college freshmen living in the dorm is to have one other roommate in a room designed for two people. Many students prefer this because it allows for an immediate new acquaintance. You then hope that the two of you get along easily and live comfortably with each other. Through this person, you are given the possibility to meet new people. It is someone to go with you to lunch, the new student picnic, or even church. Triple dorm rooms are far and few between. It may sound great to live with two other people because it gives you a better chance of meeting new faces. However, what may happen is that two of the three become good friends, leaving the third person feeling like the third wheel. While this may not happen too often, it is something to consider before deciding to live in a triple. There will be more on getting along with your roommate(s) in an upcoming section.

Sharing a bathroom at home with a sibling is one thing, but sharing it with more than twenty other people is a whole different world. Most dorms have community bathrooms, with a limited number of showers and stalls. No need to freak out. Because of everyone's different schedules, the bathrooms are rarely filled, so you hardly ever have to wait in line. When your dorm has community bathrooms, it is helpful to use a shower caddy to keep all of your toiletries in one spot. Regardless of what type of bathroom setup you have in your dorm, a caddy is always helpful. A bathrobe might also come in handy if you do not feel comfortable walking around in a towel. Most people opt to wear flip-flops in the shower.

While a community bathroom may sound scary—and a bit like an invasion of privacy—there are benefits to them. You don't need to clean the sinks or buy toilet paper. It is all done for you. College maintenance workers clean the bathrooms regularly so they are usually pretty clean . . . usually. Occasionally on weekends you will wake up to a mess, but not that often.

Those who can't handle the issues involved with community bathrooms often choose to live in a suite-style dorm. In this arrangement, you share a bathroom with your neighbors. This suite style of living has its pros and cons. The trade-off for having your own bathroom means you are responsible for its cleaning and supplies. Consider the extra costs involved in providing toilet paper, soap, and cleaning supplies. The nice thing is that you are able to personalize the bathroom to your liking and make it feel like home.

Colleges make efforts to accommodate a great variety of personality styles when it comes to on-campus living. Some buildings offer quiet study floors. Noise is kept to a minimum to ensure an ideal study environment. Other dorms are designated for athletes; these are normally located near the sports practice facilities. In many cases, athletes attending college on sports scholarships may have no housing choices. Your roommate will most likely be a teammate.

For many colleges, academic performance is very important, so they have specialized dorms for those students who meet the academic requirements for admission into honors programs. Living in an honors dorm makes it easier to find other students in one of your current or future honors classes.

If you are not an athlete, or in honors college, you generally have greater flexibility in choosing on-campus housing. Most colleges and universities designate some dorms for freshmen and others for upperclassmen. Double-check to make sure you meet the requirements for the dorm you are requesting.

Additional items to consider when selecting the right dorm for you:

- Cable and Internet hookup

- Visitation restrictions

- Air-conditioning

- Smoking restrictions

- Laundry facilities

- Elevators (or lack thereof)

- Community kitchens

- Mattress size

- Room types offered (single, double, triple)

- Location on campus

Roommate

You and your best friend have both gotten accepted into the same state university. Congratulations! Now you must decide whether to room together. Your first instinct is probably "Yes, why wouldn't we?" But there are a few things you must consider first. Think about living with this person in a small, confined space twenty-four hours a day, seven days a week, for nine months. Do you really know everything about each other? Can your friendship endure through all the late nights and the arguments over who cleaned last or who didn't lock the door? It is possible that your friendship is strong enough and that the two of you will have the best freshman year ever. The decision to room together is something the two of you need to pray about and think through, long and hard. It might be better for both of you to live with someone you do not know for the first year. You could request to live in the same building; that way the two of you can be close and know that your friend is right around the corner or only a couple of floors away. This gives you the chance to see each other's lifestyle close-up without actually living right in the middle of it. Now you know exactly what you would be getting into, and there will be no surprises next year.

Say you have decided to be assigned a random room-mate. During the summer months, you will receive his or her contact information. It is highly recommended you e-mail or phone the person and introduce yourself. Discuss move-in times and what each person is bringing as you get to know each other a little bit. This makes it less nerve-racking when you first meet and also eliminates the chance of having two televisions and no refrigerator. Girls, more likely than boys, worry about whether their color schemes and decor will complement the other. Truthfully, it really does not matter, so feel free to let your individual style show.

It is important to establish boundaries early on in the semester. You and your roommate need to be on the same page about sharing and respecting clothes, computers, television, music, DVDs, and food. Talk about whether you are going to split the room down the middle as far as keeping it clean or how you are going to share the room. Make sure that you're not the one who creates the tornado in the room and leaves stuff thrown everywhere. It is one thing to have a pile of clothes or papers on the floor, but quite another to invade your roommate's space. In return, your roommate will hopefully do the same. Some universities aid the compatibility process by requiring roommate contracts. These contracts talk about sharing possessions, bedtimes, study habits (music on or complete silence), visitors, and other boundaries.

Visitors are always welcome and can be just what you need if you are missing home. However, it is important to let your roommate know when visitors are coming and for how long. Talk about sleeping, shower, and other arrangements so that the two of you do not argue in front of your guest. If you or your roommate is gone for the weekend, either at home or visiting someone else, talk about whether it would be all right for someone else to sleep in the empty bed. Although visitors are nice to have, it is not necessary to have people over every weekend. It is important for you and your roommate to have time to get to know each other as well as to have time to yourselves. While we're on the topic of visitors, it's also important to establish early on with your roommate clear expectations regarding members of the opposite sex staying over (and we're not talking about your roommate's kid brother or sister). While this might be an uncomfortable conversation initially, it's important to clearly establish your Christian viewpoint on premarital sex with your roommate.

Walking back to my room one night, I had no idea I was about to see more of my roommate than I had ever planned on seeing. I went to high school with her, but we weren't friends in high school. We were randomly assigned as roommates. That weekend, she had one of her guy friends from high school, whom I did not know very well, come to visit. When I opened the door to our room, the light from the hallway re-

vealed the two of them naked in her bed. Stunned, all I could say was, "Oh . . . okay," as I turned around and left. I stood in the hallway for a few seconds wondering where the heck I was supposed to sleep that night. I could not call any of my friends because it was past midnight. Luckily, I could hear my neighbor's television, so I knocked on her door and asked if I could sit and watch with her for a while.

Communication is the key to a good relationship with your roommate. Cooperation, flexibility, and honesty are important to keep in mind. Let your roommate know how you feel, and do not wait to address a problem until it has spiraled out of control. This is the first step; resolving the problem by yourselves. Allow some time to see if the two of you can resolve the issue. If that does not work, ask a friend to act as a mediator. If the problem persists, consult your Resident Assistant (RA), or start the process of a roommate change if a resolution truly cannot be reached.

Dorm Food

One thing college students do not do is starve. Despite what people have always said about how awful dorm food is, the reality is that dorm food is not really that bad. It's just not always the same as what you get at home. In most cases, nearly every appetite can be satisfied. Many colleges have taken steps to provide healthier eating options such as whole-grain breads, salads, fresh fruits and vegetables, and main courses designated as the "healthy choice." Of course, most cafeterias also offer unlimited fountain-beverage machines, cookies, pizza, ice cream, and so forth. With no parents around, it's up to you to make good food choices.

Dorm dining centers are not your only options for on-campus dining. Most colleges have food courts that include restaurants such as Subway, McDonald's, and Chik-fil-A. Usually, these food courts require a payment form other than your campus dining card. Try to save the food court—and your food budget—for a special treat.

As much as you think that you are going to eat in your room, living on a diet of ramen noodles and Easy Mac, it is much easier to grab a meal in the dining center. Meal plans are set up that allow you a certain number of meals or a dollar amount per week. Take into consideration your class schedule and how much you are going to be eating in the dining centers. Some even offer to-go containers for those on a tight schedule. Lines can become long during prime lunch and dinner hours, so plan ahead as to how much time you allow yourself. Check to see if you get extra meals so that you are able to feed any visitors.

For all those aspiring chefs out there, you may not have the appliances necessary to cook your favorite gourmet meal. Dorm-room appliances are normally limited to a mini-fridge and a microwave. While your floor might be equipped with a cooktop and oven in the lounge area, these may not always be available or working properly. Learn to be creative. You might be surprised at the things that can be made using a microwave, including s'mores, puffed-rice treats, and quesadillas. When you're desperate, you will think of things and do pretty much anything to make it happen, even making a perfectly toasted grilled-cheese sandwich with your iron. We'll confess to being in such a rush one afternoon that we decided to use a hair dryer to cool off freshly baked cookies. This is definitely not how your mother would do it, but you do what you have to do to get the job done.

|||||||||||||||||||||||||||||

Activities

Getting involved is one of the most important things for your freshman year of college. You are not going to meet new people and create lifelong friendships just by sitting in your room staring at your computer screen. You will be informed about and invited to an endless amount of first-week activities on campus. Newsletters and announcements might even be mailed to your home before you leave for college. When moving in, keep an eye out for posters and bulletins with information about welcome activities and events for other organizations. Grab your roommate or a neighbor and get out there! Do not sit in your room the first weekend, and avoid the temptation to go home the first couple of weekends. It might seem scary at first, but everyone is feeling the same way. They are just as nervous and apprehensive as you are.

Your RA will announce floor activities that allow you to get to know your neighbors. Something as simple as going down for dinner with your floor is a great way to socialize. Competing against other floors in different sports and activities allows you to meet even more people, as does taking a leadership role in floor and building activities such as decorating, birthday celebrations, and recycling. Hall councils are formed to allow you, the resident, to have a say in how you want your building to be run. A variety of activities and competitions can be created between buildings. Video-game competitions are common on college campuses. Community outreach projects are also established as another great way to get involved. Going to activities provides you with the experience of meeting lots of new people. Granted, you will not become friends with every new person you meet, but the more people you do meet, the more opportunities you have to establish new friendships.

There is never a dull night on a college campus. Most universities offer organized events such as plays, concerts, comedians, clubs, and athletic events. You get to watch your fellow students in plays as well as watch well-known comedians or singers/bands perform right in front of you. As for clubs, they can be anything from academic, athletic, Greek life, religious, or other shared-cause-based clubs. These are great places to meet new people with similar interests. And don't forget to go to campus sporting events. Here you get a chance to show your school spirit and cheer student athletes on to victory.

University-organized intramurals allow you to compete in an array of sports such as volleyball, basketball, softball, tennis, and even Ping-Pong! These sports can be co-ed, same gendered, or individual. Form a team of friends, floor mates, or anyone else you can think of. You don't have to be the best athlete to be able to compete. Intramurals are a great way to socialize and be a part of a team.

Noise

BOOM, POW, CRASH, KA-PLOW, BANG! No, it's not the end of the world; it's just your next-door neighbors blasting their music again. No matter what time of night, you will always find someone awake in a college dorm. They might be in the hallway talking on their cell phones, complaining to or arguing with someone, or having a movie night in their room with the door open. Most people are respectful when it comes to noise levels, but there are those few who can be obnoxious and not be considerate of those around them. Dorm-room walls are extremely thin, and things can be heard from every which direction. Televisions, microwaves, music, and even coughing can be heard from the next room.

It is easy to get frustrated with people and their noise levels, so it is important to confront these individuals in a respectful way early on in order to resolve issues before they get out of hand. You do not want to be up studying for an important test and not be able to hear yourself think. Remember to keep in mind your own noise levels and to be respectful to your roommate and the rest of the floor. Use common sense: blow-dry your hair in the bathroom if your roommate is still sleeping, for example. If your roommate wants to go to bed early, keep on only the lights that you really need and talk on your cell phone in the lounge area.

You and/or your parents are paying plenty of money for you to attend college, so academics should be at the top of your priority list. Studying is very important if you want to succeed. The library can be one of the best places to escape the noise of the dorm. Group study rooms are available for a private area to work on homework or group projects. Most are furnished with comfy couches to relax on while reading your English book or a daily fix of gossip from the latest magazine. Studying on the weekends might seem like something you will never do, but valuable quiet time is available in the mornings and early afternoon because most of the floor will be sleeping in during this time. Make sure to use this time to your advantage.

Final exam weeks can be an extremely stressful. Colleges realize that people need noise levels reduced during this time, so most have what are known as quiet hours in the dorms. Noise levels are lowered to a minimum during all hours of the day except for a couple of relief hours during the week of finals. During this time, keep your television turned down so that someone in the hallway outside your door cannot hear it, listen to music through headphones, and use your cell phone outside. If you are loud during quiet hours, you could get written up by your RA, and no one wants that.

Because it is absolutely necessary for your safety, one noise that you have no control over is the ear-splitting fire alarm. It can be set off at any hour of the day or night without any sort of warning. Fire drills usually take place in the afternoons about twice a semester. Unfortunately, freshman dorms tend to be bothered the most by fire alarms being accidentally set off. Food gets burned in the microwave or someone, usually an intoxicated person, pulls the fire alarm in the middle of the night. The worst is to be in the shower when the alarm sounds. Most of the time, you do not have time to change, which leaves you wearing a towel outside, possibly even in the middle of winter—another reason to always wear a robe to the bathroom!

Your Faith in the Dorm

College can be one of the biggest tests to your faith. Temptations and obstacles await you around every corner. Joshua 1:9 is a fitting verse to start with when you are feeling nervous about moving away from home and need the comfort of your Lord and Savior. The Lord tells you, "Have I not commanded you? Be strong and courageous. Do not be frightened, and do not be dismayed, for the LORD your God is with you wherever you go." Knowing that God is always with you, no matter what the circumstances, can pull you through your most difficult days. Talk to Him when you're down or afraid or lonely. He knows what you're going through.

Your biggest test of faith in the dorm comes when dealing with your roommate. Unless your roommate is someone you know already, you often have no idea if your future roommate is a Christian. He or she may not share your Christian faith. You need to be understanding and respectful of your roommate's beliefs while also ensuring that he or she respects your beliefs. Don't let your roommate pressure you into thinking that getting up every Sunday morning to go to church is a dumb thing to do. It's a safe bet that you may be one of only a handful awake at 8:00 a.m. on a Sunday. Ann shared this personal experience:

I got up at 9:00 a.m. the first Sunday on campus. I had seen a church a block north of my dorm and read that they had worship at 10:45. It was even Missouri Synod Lutheran! I told my friend, whom I've known since fifth grade, and who was also a freshman with me, about it and asked if she wanted to go with me to check it out. I told my roommate the night before about my plan to get up early on Sunday. I knew that she was Catholic and even went to a Catholic high school, so I figured she might be getting up for church too. She explained to me that she had thought about going to the campus Catholic church, but had decided to see what it would be like not to go to church for a while since her parents were not able to make her go as they had done in the past. Here was my chance to witness and reach out to her, but I blew it. I did not really respond much but just let it be. Looking back now, I should have said something like, "Taking a break from church? God doesn't take breaks from you just to see what it would be like." I did not feel our relationship was at the place to say something like that though, because we had known each other for only three days, so I bit my tongue. Every Sunday, I would get up and go to church while she lay in her nice, warm, cozy bed and slept late. Later, I began filling my weeks with other events with the church's campus ministry. I did not let my roommate's decision of not going to church deter me from my decision to stay connected to the church and my faith. I believe that God fully guided me through my first year of living away from home and

in a dorm, where I was exposed to many new people with different religious beliefs than mine.

Most churches in college towns have a large number of student members. Therefore, activities, events, and Bible studies offer opportunities for you to be surrounded by fellow students who are experiencing the same challenges that face Christian students in college today. Offering an invitation to someone to go to church with you never hurt anyone. You never know when or where you will run into someone that you can invite to go with you to a church service or an event. Having a conversation with someone you just met can lead to an opportunity to witness your faith. The authors know this all too well. They met a girl in line for an event and began talking because of a mutual friend. While talking about her boyfriend about the college he was attending, they found out that she was Christian. They invited her to a picnic that the church on campus was having later that evening. From that point on, they have all been very involved with the church and its campus ministry.

College is a time to experience new things. You are on your own for the first time, living in a space that you can call your own. Your faith is not something that you want to experiment with. You want to be able to have God there to depend on during times of doubt, stress, and struggles. Our Savior invites and desires us to rely on Him.

||||||||||||||||||||||||||

A Few Additional Thoughts

Many things run through your mind when you are getting ready to leave for college. Packing can be quite time consuming; be sure not to leave everything until the last minute. While we're thinking about things to pack, consider this list of important but often forgotten things to bring:

- Fan
- Lamp
- Bookshelf
- Blanket
- Umbrella
- Boots (rain/snow)
- Alarm clock
- Stamps and stationery
- Flash drive
- Cable/Internet cords
- Dish soap and towel
- Plates, bowls, cups, and silverware
- Laundry detergent and quarters for machines
- Gym shoes and any other athletic gear
- First-aid kit and toolbox with essentials
- Thumbtacks, paper clips, transparent tape, masking tape, and stapler

And last but not least, remember your Bible!

Campus housing at each university is handled slightly differently. As you consider your housing choices, you might want to research the answers to this short list of questions before beginning your freshman year of college:

- Are you allowed to stay in the dorm during holiday breaks?

- What is the parking situation for incoming freshmen?

- Does the dorm have movable furniture?

- What furniture, if any, do you need to bring?

- Is off-campus housing available and/or allowed for underclassmen?

At the beginning of this chapter, we promised to share why we listed rule number one as "Lock your door at night." In writing this chapter, a friend shared this funny, yet true, personal story of dorm life:

In the middle of the night, I knew something was not right when I had trouble staying under my covers while I was sleeping. At 7:00 a.m., I woke up to a foot kicking me in the head, and I realized this was not a dream! There was a strange girl in my bed. Her socks were on the floor, she did not have any pants on, and she reeked of alcohol. I began shaking the girl but she would not get up. She moaned, "What are you doing in my room?" I quickly corrected her saying, "No! This is my room! Get out of my bed and into your own room!" She did not budge and whined, "This is 426." After some convincing that she was not in her actual room, she finally fell out of my bed onto the floor and crawled to the door. I pointed to her room

and handed the girl her socks. I still see the girl from time to time, and we have slowly gotten over the awkwardness. If only my roommate, who went to bed after I was asleep, had locked the door, this entire incident could have been avoided.

A.V. and A.B.

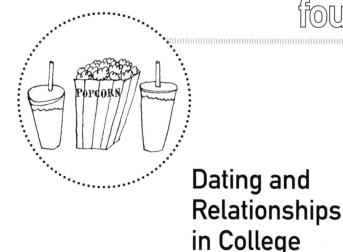

four

Dating and Relationships in College

Introduction

It seems like dating and college are synonymous nowadays. It's always the same story: boy meets girl; boy and girl hook up; boy dumps girl; boy moves on to girl's roommate. Brokenhearted girl goes out with friends to a club or party and meets new boy; girl and new boy hook up; girl dumps new boy to validate her feelings. Brokenhearted new boy meets new girl; new boy and new girl hook up; new boy dumps new girl—the cycle continues.

Yes, dating in college can be really fun, and you can meet a lot of great people and experience a lot of things while dating, but it can be very hurtful when it isn't done with care. Dating is an art form that only the brave master. This chapter will help you learn not only about dating in college but also about how to apply simple principles to your own dating life that can help you find that special someone. Hopefully, this chapter will help you see the better choices in relationships and be able to tackle the bad ones.

|||||||||||||||||||||||||||||||||

Welcome to the College Dating Scene!

College is one of the best places to meet new people. Never again in your life will you have the opportunity to be around so many people your age in the same place at the same time. Everyone is in the same place (college), has the same goals (graduation), and is completely and utterly broke. This is by far the perfect place to meet "the one" if you're careful, know what you're doing, and know what you're looking for.

Unfortunately, there are a lot of people who are ignorant as to how the actual dating process works. In high school, it was normal to start a relationship with someone just by glancing across the Bunsen burner in chemistry class. There you are, lab partners. Your eyes meet his, your lips curve into a flirtatious smile, and the band Journey starts playing quietly in the back of your mind as you imagine going to prom together. Bam! Relationship! The two of you vow to stay together forever, even after graduation. Then the summer before freshman year unfolds, and you realize that one, or both, of you wants to be "free" and feel your relationship needs to end. This usually leaves one partner in a pile of mush that is his or her broken heart.

In college, things look a whole lot different. Yes, you still have locking eyes, curving smiles, and Bunsen burners (unfortunately), but the elements of protection you had in high school are almost nonexistent. No more curfews keeping you from staying out until 2:00 a.m. No more parents waiting for you to come home at the end of your date. No more youth group, pastor, or youth leader encouraging abstinence or helping you battle temptation. Instead of relying on these outside forces to hold you accountable, you have to become (gasp!) responsible for your own actions.

When you get to college, there are more opportunities to date different people, but there are also a lot more opportunities to make mistakes. *Big* mistakes! *Catastrophic*, even! If you're not careful with your heart, you could be handing it over to someone on a silver platter, saying, "Here you go! You can cherish this or put it into an emotional blender." This is the first time in your life when you're taking complete responsibility for your actions, emotions, and spirituality. Are you ready?

Defining the Word

When I was in college, which was only a few years ago, one of the most frustrating situations that I came across was the confusion around the word *dating*. Professors don't teach you this in Freshman 101, even though you do learn a lot in biology class. Your resident adviser doesn't sit down with you to have a talk about the birds and the bees or what dating actually means. So, most freshmen enter the dating scene with a complete misunderstanding of what it actually means to date.

To clear up any further misunderstanding, the dictionary says that "to date" is "to go out on usually romantic dates." Wow, this doesn't really help a bit! Dating actually seems pretty basic. Believe it or not, dating really *is* a basic principle. Dating *basically* involves two people wanting to know each other better. They plan activities and spend time together to discover if they want to spend the rest of their lives with each other. What makes dating complicated isn't the lack of definition, it's the *people*. When you put two people of the opposite sex together, things get complicated.

From nearly the beginning of time, man and woman together have been dealing with a serious complication—sin. Yes, everything boils down to Adam and Eve. We find the happy couple in Genesis, living in Paradise. Nothing has tainted their relationship with each other or with God. They're perfect, sinless, and happy. Then the serpent comes along with his sneaky demeanor.

> *Now* the serpent was more crafty than any other beast of the field that the LORD God had made. He said to the woman, "Did God actually say, 'You shall not eat of any tree in the garden?'" And the woman said to the serpent, "We may eat of the fruit of the trees in the garden, but God said, 'You shall not eat of the fruit of the tree that is in the midst of the garden, neither shall you touch it, lest you die.'" But the serpent said to the woman, "You will not surely die. For God knows that when you eat of it your eyes will be opened, and you will be like God, knowing good and evil." Genesis 3:1–5

The serpent lies to Eve and convinces her that there's something missing in her relationship with God—knowledge. So what does Eve do? She buys into the lie, convinced that her life will be all the more better by eating this mystery fruit. She takes a bite. "So when the woman saw that the tree was good for food, and that it was a delight to the eyes, and that the tree was to be desired to make one wise, she took of its fruit and ate" (Genesis 3:6a). She doesn't stop there. Eve turned to Adam and convinced him to eat too: "She also gave some to her husband who was with her, and he ate" (Genesis 3:6b). This big, juicy bite of disaster starts the downward spiral of sin.

Here we have a woman who tries to take control, but eventually fails, and a man who's afraid to stand up for what is true and noble. Both end up feeling ashamed and guilty. Sound familiar? Because we are still tainted with sin, we are cursed with complicated relationships. Definitions are muddled, manipulation begins, and feelings get hurt, leading to scarred and bleeding hearts.

While the definition of dating should be pretty simple, it could be clarified a little more. It's true that people complicate the world of relationships, but if we can clear up some confusion as to how far dating should or should not go, maybe this could help prevent relationship disaster. Adam and Eve may have started sin, but God's grace covers this sin with salvation. Our actions are no longer ruled by Law but by the love that God has given us through His Son. Even the *basic* principle of dating can be a reflection of this love. So let's unmuddle and clear up some misconceptions of what dating actually is.

‖‖‖‖‖‖‖‖‖‖‖‖‖‖‖‖‖‖‖‖‖‖‖‖‖
Breaking Down the Definition

As the world grows older and time goes on, dating gets more complicated. Even though the idea of dating is relatively new, fifty years ago, a date would include a '57 Chevy, two teenagers, and a drive-in movie theater. The guy would pay, and the girl wouldn't mind. Opening doors and pulling out chairs was customary, and women cherished being *cherished*. After going on a few more dates, the guy would normally ask the girl's parents permission for their daughter's hand in marriage. Of course, men and woman lived different lives back then. Although life was not as challenging, it was complicated in different ways.

Nowadays, dating seems to need a clearer definition. To help explain these new definitions, let's take a look at three different ways to date: Recreational Dating, Missionary Dating, and Intentional Dating.

Recreational Dating

Recreational dating is pretty much what it sounds like. Dating for recreation. No serious attachment, just fun! Neither individual in the relationship has any intention of commitment or marriage. They're just in it for entertainment and the joy of being with that particular person . . . until they get sick of each other and move on to someone else.

Being someone who was constantly devouring spiritual literature about dating and not dating in high school, I entered college with a pretty solid belief that dating had intentional purposes only. I believed entering a relationship just for fun was absolutely not appropriate. Dating is serious business. You don't date someone who you don't want to marry. Period! As I concluded my college career and am now in the real world, my beliefs have changed slightly.

Recreational dating is what is often depicted on television. Most relationships on television seem to begin out of thin air. Two people find each other physically attractive, so they end up having sex and begin a relationship. The goal isn't commitment or marriage but how long they can actually stay together without fighting or breaking up. It seems so easy, so normal. Viewers, most of them adolescents, assume this is what dating is supposed to look like. They see relationships with no worries, no commitment, and no attachment. Whenever something goes wrong, or when one party no longer feels love for the other, the relationship ends, leaving someone (usually the girl) feeling inadequate, hurt, and brokenhearted.

Now, recreational dating is not *always* bad, but it can be dangerous. There are even some aspects about this kind of dating that are positive. Recreational dating can offer individuals the opportunity to discover who they are attracted to and what they're looking for in a mate. Is the individual attracted to athletic guys or musician-types? What is it like dating a Christian? They may ask themselves, "What am I like in a relationship?" "Am I a giver or a taker?" While questions such as these can be answered in romantic relationships, they can also be answered in platonic friendships. The danger in discovering these things while dating someone recreationally is the emotional and physical bond you can carelessly create with that person, which can lead to a broken heart.

There's always a risk whenever any two individuals start a romantic relationship. You're giving a part of yourself for that person to discover, even if it's casual. There's a little bit of your heart that goes into any relationship, especially romantic ones. Most of the time when two people begin a non-committed relationship like this, one side is more invested emotionally than the other. When you have the impression that your partner is on the same page as you, he or she might want more. This kind of miscommunication creates terrible broken hearts. When someone else's heart is on the line, it's so important to have clear communication behind your intentions. Are both parties willing to sacrifice their hearts and part of themselves for a noncommittal relationship?

There are some people who realize that this relationship is completely casual and there's no commitment involved. No strings attached, just for fun. "We'll see how things go."

When both parties are on the same page and completely understand that their relationship is casual, this can be a lot of fun. But the majority of the time, it doesn't really work out in the end. One person is always hurt and upset because he or she thought there was something more, while the other is confused as to how the other could assume this.

A better alternative for this kind of dating is just plain friendship. Two friends are able to have fun together without being in a romantic relationship. You can discover a lot of things about yourself and others by interacting with them one-on-one or on a group date. Sometimes you can see more things in your friend that you wouldn't be able to see if in a romantic relationship. This kind of friendship can be a positive experience for both parties without the added frustration of being romantic and the temptations that accompany that kind of relationship.

Missionary Dating

Like recreational dating, missionary dating can have dangerous consequences. Missionary, or evangelism, dating is dating for the sake of saving a soul. Some Christians feel the need to reach others spiritually through a dating relationship rather than friendship. They become romantically involved because of an initial attraction, but they continue the relationship for evangelism purposes. I've seen many college-aged Christians approach an unhealthy relationship with the idea that they will *save* their partner through a romantic relationship, only to find themselves in a frustrating battle of faith or heartbroken from an ugly breakup.

Now, evangelism should be the heartbeat of every Christian. In the Great Commission, Jesus directs us to "Go therefore and make disciples of all nations, baptizing them in the name of the Father and of the Son and of the Holy Spirit, teaching them to observe all that I have commanded you" (Matthew 28:19–20). Jesus directs us to reach nonbelievers with the Gospel, the truth. As Christians, we are called to spread the message of Christ to those who are sick and broken. The Great Commission reminds us of the freedom we have as believers to share the love of Christ with others. By establishing relationships with all people, all nations, we are able to reach the world.

Even though the relationships we have with those around us are essential to spreading God's Word, it can be spiritually dangerous to enter a romantic relationship with someone who's a nonbeliever. "Do not be unequally yoked with unbelievers. For what partnership has righteousness with lawlessness? Or what fellowship has light with darkness?" (2 Corinthians 6:14). When we are yoked with unbelievers, we are sharing our lives with people who have chosen to reject God and deny His love. As people of faith and righteousness, we put ourselves in a dangerous situation by becoming vulnerable to the actions of those who do not know the love of Christ. Just like recreational dating, you take a great risk evangelizing to someone in this kind of relationship. Instead of risking your heart, you could be risking your very faith.

I want to share a story with you about my friend Mary. Even though she's a little older than me, she has an incredible story to tell about dating a nonbeliever and some of the consequences that may come from diving into such a dangerous situation head first.

Mary grew up going to church. Even though her walk with God may have faltered throughout the years, her faith was still strong. In college, Mary struggled with being a Christian at a secular university. She valued her relationship with God and other Christians, but it seemed to her as though she had dated all the Christian guys and there was no one left that interested her. So she decided that she would start to date non-Christians, even though she knew that it might be dangerous spiritually to get seriously involved. Mary's faith may have been strong, but her actions, especially in her dating world, did not reflect what was on her heart. Mary eventually graduated from college unmarried and still looking for Mr. Right.

A few months after graduation, while bowling with some friends, Mary met Paul. He was older than her, handsome, tall, and had a killer smile. She sent him a coy smile and he reciprocated with a flirty wink. Quickly their innocent flirtation became an interesting conversation: common interests, favorite musical groups, movies they hated, past relationships, and the desire to settle down and start a family. Paul was fascinated by Mary's bold opinions, Mary soon learned of Paul's family, and his age, ten years her senior.

Mary and Paul were smitten. Their whirlwind romance seemed to have been written by the hand of fate. Mary and Paul quickly became a serious couple headed for marriage. After being together for only three weeks, Paul proposed. Mary happily said "yes," but she had hesitations.

Paul was a non-Christian. He had grown up in a Lutheran home, but had fallen away from his faith. Mary really struggled with his spirituality, but hoped that she could bring the love of Christ to him through their marriage. Paul promised Mary that he would be open to going to church with her. If they had children, he would be at their Baptism. He would watch them sing in the church choir or Christmas programs, and he would see them get married in a church. According to Mary, Paul was very open to the Holy Spirit and made promises to attend church. She knew that God could work in their marriage because of this, but she still was unsure.

She asked her friends and family what they thought of her decision to marry Paul, and each had differing opinions. Her Christian friends advised against it. They thought it was foolish of her to marry a nonbeliever because of the vulnerable position she'd be putting herself in. He would discourage her spiritually and eventually her faith could suffer from it. Her family members were of a different opinion. They knew that the Holy Spirit could work in many different ways, but there was also the possibility that if Mary didn't marry Paul, he could marry a nonbeliever and never hear the Gospel again. Mary's relationship with Paul could possibly lead him back to the Church and eventually back to a living and active faith.

Mary not only struggled with Paul's spirituality but also with her feelings of security. Paul was a civil-case lawyer at his own private firm, so Mary knew she would be financially set for the rest of her life. This good and moral man might not be a Christian, but he could provide a good life for her and their future family. Eventually, Mary chose to marry Paul, putting her need for security above her walk with the Lord.

Fast-forward twenty-three years. Mary and Paul are still married and have two beautiful girls in college, but their marriage is filled with unhappiness, guilt, and regret. At first, Paul had fulfilled some of his promises to Mary about attending church. He was present at their daughters' Baptisms and attended the occasional Christmas and Easter worship service. But after a few years of "paying his dues," he stopped going completely. Now Paul is an atheist, completely frustrated with Mary's growing faith and involvement in church.

Mary is also frustrated with her relationship with her husband. The connection they once had as husband and wife is no longer there. Mary says that she has major regrets about marrying her husband. If she could erase time, she would go back and marry a Christian, someone who shares her faith and is bonded with Christ. Neither Mary nor Paul believes in divorce. Paul has never hurt Mary physically, and to her knowledge, he has always been faithful, so there is no reason in God's eyes they should get divorced. It is apparent that Paul continues their marriage for financial reasons.

As Mary told me her story, I could see the death of their marriage in the words she used. Regret. Disappointment. Hurt. The two no longer had a marriage or a common bond of love and respect. They were just two people living in the same house. Even though their daughters are Christians, Mary can see the spiritual battle they endure because of their parents.

Mary sees her mistake every day and lives with the consequences of marrying a non-Christian, but her faith has not wavered. She is stronger in her faith now more than ever and strives in her spiritual walk. Mary is a wonderful example of perseverance and God's mysterious workings. She has a quiet confidence in her that shows where her faith lies, in Christ. Although she may have regrets about her marriage, she has risen above it and has become a mighty servant who is saved by grace.

This story may seem like a drastic situation, but in reality, it's often what happens when someone begins a relationship with a nonbeliever. Unfortunately, there are many Christians who have the same hope as Mary, that they can reach their boyfriend or girlfriend with the Gospel through a romantic relationship. The truth is that it's easier for a non-Christian to bring a Christian down in his or her faith than for a Christian to successfully evangelize to a nonbeliever. As St. Paul put it, "Bad company ruins good morals" (1 Corinthians 15:33b). This does not mean, however, that you cannot evangelize through friendships. Just as Christ spread the truth to all around Him through relational ministry, we too can bring the Gospel to people through friendship.

Intentional Dating

Unlike recreational dating, intentional dating is dating with a purpose. Both parties understand that they are in a romantic relationship with an outcome—marriage. "Therefore a man shall leave his father and his mother and hold fast to his wife, and they shall become one flesh" (Genesis 2:24). Dating can be really fun in this kind of setting. There's freedom to discover who your partner is with the comfort in understanding a common goal, whether that's marriage or ending the relationship. If this person doesn't fit your specific standards, then the relationship ends. Just like any other romantic relationship, it's important to have a standard of what you're looking for before you enter—we'll get to that later in the chapter.

There's nothing wrong with dating at all, but it should be with a purpose, and ultimately that purpose is marriage. When a swimmer gets in the water for a race, he has a goal: to be the fastest person for 500 meters. The race starts, and he swims his hardest. When he finally finishes, he's either rewarded or disappointed. Just as a swimmer or runner knows the goal of racing, so you should know the goal of dating. The goal is marriage, but there can be a reward (the proposal) or a disappointment (breaking up).

The important thing to remember in any relationship is how your faith is reflected. "'All things are lawful,' but not all things are helpful. 'All things are lawful,' but not all things build up" (1 Corinthians 10:23). We have the freedom to act in any way we choose, whether that's deciding whom we're going to marry or what kind of cereal we want to eat in the morning. Everything is allowed, but not everything we do is helpful, especially for our faith. As Christians, we have the freedom to marry non-Christians, but we should consider if doing so would be helpful to our relationship with God. Christ died for the mistakes we make, but that doesn't necessarily mean that we can act in any way we want because we're covered by the safety net of grace.

Dating can be very complicated, especially because emotions are at stake. Paul reminds us in Philippians that whatever we do, we should think about what's praiseworthy: "Finally, brothers, whatever is true, whatever is honorable, whatever is just, whatever is pure, whatever is lovely, whatever is commendable, if there is any excellence, if there is anything worthy of praise, think about these things" (4:8). This is a great guideline for the relationships you have with others, whether romantic or platonic. Whatever is true, honorable, just, pure, lovely, or commendable, surround yourself with these things.

IIIIIIIIIIIIIIIIIIIIIIIIIIII
How to Date 101

Now that you know all about healthy types of dating, you might be wondering *how* to date someone. On a basic level, dating is all about asking and being asked, but in recent years some confusion has developed as to *who* should be doing what. A fine balance exists for both guys and girls as they learn their roles in the dating process. Many so-called experts express views and theories about who should ask whom and gender roles. Sometimes you just need to discover for yourself what works best when dating. For now, I'm going to teach you about football and chess.

Football

The game of football is very fast-paced. You have two teams beating on each other mercilessly until the ball goes into one end zone to score a touchdown. Each team tries to score some points to win the game. You have a winner and a loser. There's strategy and a set of plays (or guidelines) for the players, but when push comes to shove, if a play doesn't work out, the quarterback has to be able to think on his feet. Football is rough and quick, with strategy and goals.

Dating can be the same way. "Football" daters are very fast-paced. They don't sit on the sidelines waiting to ask someone out or to be asked; they get in the game and pursue boldly. For example: Jerry meets Jenny in Chemistry 101. Jerry thinks Jenny is cute and funny, so he asks her out to a movie on Friday night. They have a great time and by the following Monday, Jerry and Jenny are dating exclusively. This may seem very quick to some, but this kind of dating works for Jerry and Jenny. Jerry does a lot of thinking on his feet but still has a strategy. He knows that Jenny has qualities he's looking for in a wife and wants to discover who she is as soon as he can. Jerry has a goal to get the girl and a strategy of how to make that happen—ask her out. Even though he pursues boldly, risking being hurt, he is able to be flexible along the way.

Playing football is an aggressive dating strategy. Sometimes people who play the dating game like this break a lot of hearts in a hurry. This is where the importance of intentional dating comes in. Until both parties share the same intentions concerning marriage, playing football can be dangerously destructive.

Some who date this way want to score as many touchdowns as they can, only pursuing the physical part of the relationship. This kind of person plays carelessly with hearts, demonstrating no respect for the other person in the relationship. Because of the quick nature of the game when dating this way, you may not have enough time to discover who you're playing football with. Then it's sometimes necessary and appropriate to call "time-outs" in your relationship to take things slower.

Playing football works well for people who are bold, know exactly what they want, and are flexible enough to think on their feet. Most of the time, these people are spontaneous and like to live in the moment. Unfortunately, people who date this way may not have the patience to guard their partner's heart, or their own for that matter. Because of this, it's very important for a couple to consciously slow down and be patient in getting to know each other. When a couple goes too fast, serious emotional and physical consequences may result. When there's not enough time to stop and think about decisions logically, hearts can get broken. Unless you're prepared to play big and possibly lose big, you might be better off dating another way. For those people who may want to take things a little slower and logically think about their decisions, you might consider another option.

Chess

Chess is a thinking game, involving patience and control. Instead of a rowdy, fast-paced, bruise-bearing game like football, chess is played with complete thought, organization, and strategy. Chess moves much slower, but there's still a winner, a loser, and great strategy. The players don't rush into decisions; they think about them with care and ease. Players have an idea of where the other player might make the next move and respond appropriately. This game is still very aggressive, but players have more time to think about their next move and play the game right.

People who date this way are very strategic and patient. Looking at our favorite football-playing couple, we see that Jerry and Jenny act very differently when they date like playing chess. Jerry still meets Jenny in Chemistry 101, but instead of asking her out right away, he allows the relationship to become a friendship first. He still spends time with Jenny but works more strategically and slowly to make their relationship exclusive. He finds out about Jenny's reputation by asking his friends about her. Jerry sees how she interacts with her friends and others and observes her relationship with God. This might take a while, but Jerry's willing to put in the time and effort to make sure this girl is someone he really could see himself in a committed relationship with—possibly marriage. After Jerry finds out about Jenny, and they have spent time together, he asks Jenny to be in an exclusive relationship, and she agrees.

Playing chess can be a very slow-moving game. Sometimes people who date like playing chess move *too* slowly and eventually the person they're spending time with loses interest and moves on to someone else. There's a fine balance the chess player must learn. Strategy is very important when playing chess, but you still need to *play*. When it appears like you quit the game too early, you'll lose the interest of the other person.

Playing chess can be a really fun way to date. There's a lot of time for wooing and reciprocation. Instead of quickly blowing over the first part of the relationship, there's more time to cherish the little things. When two people play chess as opposed to football, there's more time to discover each other. Simple dates or acts of affection become the highlight of your time together. Just sitting next to each other spurs excitement and anticipation for the next part of the relationship. Hearts can be guarded more easily and there's more opportunity to communicate intentions before the relationship becomes too serious too soon. Again, chess dating is not for everyone. It takes lots of patience and self-control to date this way, but there are many rewards for taking it slow.

Knowing how to guard your partner's heart with respect and love is very important in having a successful relationship. "Keep your heart with all vigilance, for from it flow the springs of life" (Proverbs 4:23). Our emotions and feelings are tightly woven together with our hearts and desires. When we are careless with our own hearts, or are not careful with someone else's, we can cause serious damage without even knowing it. Regular wear and tear on the heart may not seem painful, but after time, too much heartbreak or carelessness causes a heart to break more easily. It's normal to experience rejection or heartbreak throughout your life, especially in junior high or high school. Most people learn from their romantic mistakes and can be strengthened by heartbreak. However, there are some people who cannot glean positive lessons from their hurt.

When someone is unable to guard his or her heart appropriately, that person could place his or her heart in the wrong person's hands. One breakup or inappropriate relationship might result in an unhealthy view on dating and marriage altogether.

Dating can be fun and should lead to marriage, but those who don't guard their hearts could sacrifice themselves to a life filled with unhappiness and loneliness. No matter how you play the dating game, whether it's football or chess, you need to guard some hearts, especially your own.

||||||||||||||||||||||||

Don't Worry So Much!

There's a lot of pressure to date in college. For people in close-knit, Christian communities, there seems to be an even greater pressure to get married. It's very easy to get caught up in the dating scene, always wondering who "the one" is going to be. Instead of worrying so much about how to date the right way or who you're going to marry—or *if* you're going to get married—remember that God has it all in control.

> *Therefore* I tell you, do not be anxious about your life, what you will eat or what you will drink, nor about your body, what you will put on. Is not life more than food, and the body more than clothing? Look at the birds of the air: they neither sow nor reap nor gather into barns, and yet your heavenly Father feeds them. Are you not of more value than they? And which of you by being anxious can add a single hour to his span of life? Matthew 6:25–27

Just like the flowers in the fields, God takes care of you. Worrying about relationships is futile, especially because God says He will take care of us in everything we do. When we worry, we add more age lines to our faces without the bonus of wisdom. Besides, if you worry too much, you could worry yourself right out of a relationship. When it comes to dating, God will make it happen.

||||||||||||||||||||||||

Picking "The One"

Whenever I talk to college students about dating, one question always comes up: "How will I know he/she's the one?" I share the same answer that I've heard from every married couple, "You just *know*!" Thanks a lot. Not very helpful. Even though you may not know how to tell who the one is yet, I hope to shed some light on how to get a little closer.

Filet Mignon

I don't really have many opportunities to eat out at really nice restaurants, especially on a church worker's salary. However, when I do have a chance to go to one of those restaurants with ten forks, five courses, and a cheese cart, I always order the best thing on the menu. Of course, we all know that the *best* thing on the menu is filet mignon. This French classic is delicate to the palate and offers heady aromas straight from a four-star grill. So, I order my filet mignon with joy and wait . . . patiently.

The thing about filet mignon is that it takes a while to prepare. It's not like KFC or McDonald's, where you can order through an automatic-closing window and get your food in 2.5 minutes. No, it takes patience for the chef to prepare *my* filet mignon to its finest, the way I like it. So, I wait.

Picking "the one" is like ordering filet mignon. You want to marry the best person for you, your filet mignon. That person's qualities match your palate perfectly—he or she completes you perfectly, bringing out your best qualities.

You know you want the filet mignon, but you have to wait . . . patiently. Sure, it would be easier to run out to a fast-food restaurant and order something lickety-split, but it's not going to be the *best* thing. You want the best thing. God wants the best for you. Don't lower your standards for something easier or faster or *right here*. Be patient—it'll be worth the wait.

Bubble Boys and Girls

Patience may not be a problem for you, but you might not even know *what* you're looking for. What does your filet mignon look like? We're going to do an activity together to help us learn about filet mignon. First, we need to make a Bubble Boy/Girl.

Here is a circle. Right now, you have the opportunity to discover what kind of standards you have for your future husband or wife. First, you'll need a writing utensil. A pencil is easier to erase, so you can change your mind as much as you want. Next, fill in your empty circle, or bubble, with all the qualities you're looking for in a spouse. Not a boyfriend or girlfriend, but a hus- band or wife! This is *very* impor- tant! Go ahead, start filling in. I want you to put *anything* in there. It can be as shallow or as deep as you want it to be. You're the only person who's going to see this . . . as long as you don't lend out this book.

Your Bubble Boy/Girl

Hopefully, this activity will give you some kind of idea of what your filet mignon looks like. The hard part isn't writing in the bubble, it's sticking with the standard! Always remem- ber that God has your heart in the palm of His hand. He's with you and singing over you. "The LORD your God is in your midst, a mighty one who will save; He will rejoice over you with gladness; He will quiet you by His love; He will exult over you with loud singing" (Zephaniah 3:17). You may get discouraged in trying to find your filet mignon or Bubble Boy/Girl, but remember that God is with you each step of the way.

|||||||||||||||||||||||||||||

Sex

We've already talked about defining the word *dating* and two different ways people choose to intentionally date. But no matter how you choose to date, there's always temptation that comes with being in a romantic relationship with someone—sex.

Believe it or not, there is sex in college. Even if you attend the most conservative Christian university on earth, where boys and girls aren't even allowed to *look* at each other, there's always someone sneaking off in the middle of the day for sex. It's an inevitable consequence of our sinful condition. You can turn your head, avert your eyes, and completely ignore the fact, but sex is happening on every college campus in every state in America.

The good news is that not *everyone* is having sex. More than ever, students are choosing abstinence. These people aren't just the dorky Bible-thumping Christians—they're smart and very cool students. The pressure to have sex may be there, but these students are committed to saving sex until marriage. In fact, abstinence is a whole lot healthier than the alternative . . . which reminds me of raw chicken.

Raw Chicken

When I was in college, I had the privilege of taking Honors Cultural Anthropology with Dr. Shultz. This mighty man, towering high above my five-foot-three-inch frame, gave me a lot of insight into life outside of our little bubble of college.

One day in the middle of the semester, Dr. Shultz opened up his class discussion to include the metaphor of raw chicken. I am privileged to share it with you today.

It is not illegal to eat raw chicken. There is no law that says a person can't eat raw chicken. Sure, there are laws that prohibit established restaurants from serving raw chicken, but if you were to go to your local grocery store, buy a six-pack of chicken breasts, and scarf them down without cooking them, you wouldn't be put into jail or be given a fine.

But I'm warning you, there are consequences. As we all know, if you eat raw chicken, chances are that you're going to get sick. Salmonella bacteria can cause serious damage to your body. When you consume some raw foods, such as raw chicken, your chances of being contaminated with this bacterium increase exponentially.

If you're hungry for some chicken, the best way to eat it would be *after* cooking. If you patiently wait for your boneless, skinless chicken breast to cook thoroughly, it can actually be very healthy for you. Many doctors and nutritionists advise people trying to gain muscle mass or to lose weight to eat more lean meats such as boneless, skinless chicken breast. But this tasty treat is only healthy if you allow it to cook properly.

Sex before marriage is like eating raw chicken. There are no laws against sex before marriage. In fact, almost everything in our society tells us that it's *better* for you to have sex before you're married. The sinful world says practice makes perfect, right? So, go ahead! Have sex!

But the world forgets to mention the consequences. Having sex before marriage is just like eating raw chicken; you can become really sick. Not only can you get physically sick with sexually transmitted diseases, such as HIV, chlamydia, or crabs, but you can get emotionally and spiritually sick as well. When you have sex before you're married, it can be very emotionally painful when that relationship, be it a one-night stand or a two-year romance, is broken.

Spiritually speaking, just like any other sin, sex before marriage causes some serious spiritual damage. When you're having sex with someone who's not your husband or wife, you're causing a serious rift between yourself and God. This gift of sex is just that, a *gift*. God created our bodies. He blessed us with the gift of sex. Yet, when that gift is not used within the context of marriage, this sinful act creates distance and separation from God.

Thankfully, this damage does not have to be permanent. As Christians, we know that the damage can only be undone through the blood of Christ shed for us at the cross. You are forgiven completely. God's gift of grace covers you and gives you eternal life. As Paul reminds us, we are not free to go on sinning; rather we need to live according to the will of God (Romans 6:1–2).

Patience is a key ingredient when waiting for your chicken to cook, but when you're ready and you have made the commitment of marriage, sex is God's gift to connect a husband and wife in a lifelong way. Two people literally become one. "Therefore a man shall leave his father and his mother and hold fast to his wife, and the two shall become one flesh" (Matthew 19:5). Wait for that chicken to cook and everyone will be a lot healthier and happier.

|||||||||||||||||||||||||||

Submission

The word *submission* has grown to be taboo in today's society. We seem to assume that being submissive is about being passive or laying down our rights and opinions. I remember reading Ephesians 5:22 when I was in high school: "Wives, submit to your own husbands, as to the Lord." As a result, I really struggled with my role as a woman in the Church. My very nature, my personality, is so much rooted in being passionately independent. I had this mental picture of a quiet, agreeable wife, always siding with her husband, no arguments ever spoken. The thought shook me to my spiritual core. God and I had some words about this passage on many occasions, mostly me voicing my frustrations with this idea of being passive.

As I've grown in my relationship with my Creator, I've come to realize that being submissive isn't about being passive. In fact, these concepts are completely opposite. Submission has more to do with respect than anything else. If I had read all of Ephesians 5, my misunderstandings would have been corrected very quickly: "Submitting to one another out of reverence for Christ," (v. 21). God not only tells man and woman to submit to each other but He also says that this is essential for the Christian Church.

In every relationship we are involved in, whether dating or just spending time together, we are called to submit to one another out of respect and love for God. It's not about being walked on or being a doormat. It's about the sacrificial love Christ showed us on the cross. When we submit to one another in relationships, we place the well-being of the other person above our own, serving that person in our daily life. When we adopt the mentality of respect and sacrifice for others, we are showing them the very essence of God's love for us.

The act of submission is very difficult and cannot be mastered alone. In our human sinfulness, we are completely unable to give that kind of love to others. We always end up messing things up in our selfish desires or pride. The good news is that God is there, submitting *for* us.

Paul says to the Church in Corinth, "For the sake of Christ, then, I am content with weaknesses, insults, hardships, persecutions, and calamities. For when I am weak, then I am strong" (2 Corinthians 12:10). God fills in our weaknesses and our gaps with His strength.

There are days when the last thing we want to do is submit to our friend, roommate, or boy/girlfriend, and we try to think of any excuse to keep from doing so. Yet, in our weak inability to submit, God carries us and strengthens us in our actions. Yes, we mess things up, but His grace covers our mistakes through the sacrificial love of the Lamb. The best we can do is to *not do* anything at all.

One Last Thing

Dating in college can be a really great experience if you're intentional and adopt healthy habits in your relationships. God blesses us every day with wonderful people who can show us who He is. Being in a romantic relationship can open our eyes to a different Savior than we've seen before, practicing unconditional love and forgiveness. God gives us the freedom to explore who we are by interacting with other people, but He also gives us guidelines to be able to balance a healthy relationship romantically.

Some people meet that special someone they'll spend the rest of their life with during freshman orientation. Others date several people or nobody at all in their college career.

Whatever happens during those four to six years of college, we have the opportunity to shine the light of Christ in those relationships. Ephesians 5:1–2 says, "Therefore be imitators of God, as beloved children. And walk in love, as Christ loved us and gave Himself up for us, a fragrant offering and sacrifice to God." Christian students represent Christ in all they do, whether in a relationship or single. You have the opportunity to show others the love of Christ in your daily life, to exude Him and imitate His salvation in Jesus. "In this is love, not that we have loved God but that He loved us and sent His Son to be the propitiation for our sins. Beloved, if God so loved us, we also ought to love one another" (1 John 4:10–11). Whatever you do, do it out of love, just as Christ loved us.

 K.P.

The Late-Night Social Scene

When I first visited Charleston to tour Eastern Illinois University, I felt that there should have been a huge sign that said, "Welcome to Collegetown, USA."

In my mind, what I saw was your stereotypical college town. I could compare it to the university burger with a side of small Midwest-town fries. It seemed to be a town that lived off the college, rather than a town that happened to have a university in it.

One of the largest employers in the town is the university. In a half-mile radius from campus, all housing is geared toward student living.

My mom and I drove down the main drag from school toward the downtown square. Near campus, rundown houses with beer cans littering overgrown lawns fronted both sides of the street. I noticed something that made me chuckle—slanting front porches furnished with dilapidated couches and skuzzy-looking recliners on which the residents could easily while away an afternoon.

The town was rather empty and spookily quiet on this hot day in early August. A few summer-school students were around. But for the most part, it was a ghost town.

We continued to make our way into town. Farther down the street, stately Victorian-era houses bordered each side. So, this is where more of the town's residents lived. The lawns were tidy and well-manicured. There was one white mansion that stood out. It had three huge, two-story-tall pillars majestically covering its grand front door entrance. A few Greek letters hung on a sign out front.

This must be a fraternity house, I thought.

Welcome to Collegetown, USA

A few weeks later, my mother dropped me off to start my first semester as a sophomore at Eastern. I was alone and on my own. For many freshmen who go away to school, this is their first taste of independence. Similarly, your parents will soon drop you off to begin the next chapter of your life—college. This may be the first time you will be completely on your own.

You will be *alone*!

Finally, *freedom*!

No more curfews set by your parents. No more threats of grounding or loss of privileges. No more need to call and tell where you are, who you are with, and what you are doing. You draw your first sigh of relief; you are your own boss. The first few days may be spent sticking close to your dorm or on campus. You will probably take a bit to adjust to your new surroundings. But soon you may get an itch to go exploring. What will you do with your free time on the weekends?

There is so much out there and so many opportunities. Or you could stay in the dorm and chill out.

Or you may want to go out and PARTY!

This simple, five-letter word is some students' sole reason for going to college. They live to hang out with friends, drink, and blow through the college years. Some students like it so much they list it as one of their top interests or hobbies on Facebook. (They might want to reconsider this if they plan on getting a reputable job or into grad school after college.)

Some students may party five days a week or more; others may limit it to the weekends or a few nights a week. Whatever the situation, this little word can hold serious repercussions. On the other hand, partying can be great fun if done in a safe, legal, and Christlike manner.

The social scene in college is very different from the high school setting, where some students party and drink, but they are still under the watchful eye of parents. College is a whole new ball game with new rules (or no rules). You may still be underage, but parent stipulations no longer apply. You are your own boss. With this new liberty, you are bound to run into the party scene sooner or later, whether you like it or not. For many, the party scene becomes a highlight of their time away at school.

While the party scene varies from campus to campus, it usually involves the abuse of alcohol. Some get so carried away, while living to party and have a good time, that they let important time and opportunities pass them by. I guess they were too busy with their heads in the toilet to even notice. The whole party atmosphere and culture even has its own days of the week to capitalize on the "fun": Messed-up Mondays, Trashed Tuesdays, Wasted Wednesdays, and Thirsty

Thursdays. Friday and Saturday have their own potty mouth versions, but cynically they offer Sober Sundays. Maybe we should be grateful that the college population and America in general still holds some respect for the Lord's day of rest.

To spice it up more, there are themed parties too—the predictable toga party, black light and highlighter parties, and duct-tape parties (where you can wear items made only of duct tape). There are Beer Olympics for those who love to make a sport out of drinking. And don't forget the whole no-clothes genre—the ABC Party (Anything But Clothes). My personal favorite has to be the Ugly Sweater Party. These parties usually occur around the holidays. Attendees go to thrift stores or raid a relative's closet to find the most hideous Christmas sweater they can find. The best ones have battery-powered light bulbs.

|||||||||||||||||||||||||||||||

Go Greek?

Greek fraternities and sororities hold the reputation of being some of the most active partiers on campuses across the country. Many believe students join Greek organizations simply to have a good time and find new friends. No matter what your viewpoint, being part of a Greek organization usually involves parties, many of which are themed and hosted by neighboring sororities and fraternities.

Deciding whether to "go Greek" is a personal decision. Greek life has many positive benefits and introduces you to new people whom you may not otherwise meet. No matter what, be aware that there are often more temptations when you join a Greek social organization. I know—I joined one!

Being a sophomore transfer student at Eastern put me in an interesting situation. I was not a new freshman like the majority of people on my residence hall floor, nor was I a traditional junior transfer student coming in from a community college. Given my unique circumstance, I considered joining a sorority. I was the Greek-life reporter for the college newspaper my first semester, so I saw most of the philanthropic side of Greek life. Still, I was curious to see what the social side was like.

So, I pledged to a sorority in the spring. Immediately, I was welcomed in. New social circles opened as I was invited to different functions and parties. One of the first events was at a local bar, where I saw underaged students openly drinking in the reserved back room. It was not a crazy event, but it was the first time I was offered a beer while underage in a public place.

In the end, I decided not to join the sorority because I felt no connection with the other girls. Being part of their organization would consume too much of my time and resources. I was not ready to make the commitment. I am happy for it because I would not have stayed close to some of the other wonderful Christian friends I met along the way.

Liquid Temptations

No matter if you go to a private or public college, a conservative or liberal university, or if you go Greek or not, there will be a party scene. Parties may be held in the residence hall with booze snuck in through a third-story window, at an off-campus apartment with a keg, at a house close to campus, or even in local bars.

Parties and keggers offer students of all ages the temptation of extremely cheap and unlimited alcohol and entertainment. The music blasts, and young people fill every niche of hopping house parties. There may even be a live band. The air is often hot, sticky, and stuffy.

An open basement or cellar is the worst because of even tighter conditions and limited airflow. But for many, it does not matter. Once the alcohol loosens you up and the beat starts going, all you want to do is dance, socialize, or play drinking games.

At many house parties, you pay five bucks for a cup at the door and consume all the alcohol you want until it runs out. Kegs are usually the main drink of choice, but you can sometimes find a huge punch bowl or five-gallon containers filled with jungle juice (hard alcohol mixed with some fruit-flavored drink). Some students claim that parties provide opportunities to socialize and meet new people. Most just come to drink and have fun, claiming they need to get drunk to have a good time.

Beyond the temptation and peer pressure to party, binge drinking is a major pitfall for many college students. Binge drinking results in getting drunk quickly. For some students, it seems binge drinking is their way of proving their strength, stamina, or tolerance. Drinking games like flippy cup, beer pong, quarters, and numerous others aim to get you drunk quickly. Shots and beer bongs accomplish the same thing. But the appeal of games and the encouragement of friends backfires when you binge drink. While your body may enjoy the immediate effects, the next morning's hangover lies ahead. So on top of losing control of your drinking, you end up wasting another whole day just lying around, recovering from the effects of last night's "fun." Beyond the obvious risk of a severe hangover, the abuse of alcohol can cause you to say and do things you might never do if sober. Worse yet, binge drinking can leave you in a state where you can be taken advantage of, or it can land you in the ER with alcohol poisoning.

It seems the temptation to drink too much has been around since Noah's time, perhaps even before. Genesis 9:18–23 records a time Noah fell into temptation.

Yes, even Noah, the legendary man of faith, fell into the sin of abusing alcohol. After the flood, he planted a vineyard and reaped too many of its benefits. Noah ended up drunk, passed out, and naked in his tent. The response of Noah's sons to his drunken condition would affect future generations.

But the Bible gives us more than stories of drunken abuses. Paul encourages young Timothy to "flee youthful passions and pursue righteousness, faith, love, and peace, along with those who call on the Lord from a pure heart" (2 Timothy 2:22). In his letter to the church at Ephesus, Paul suggests an alternative to the abuse of alcohol: "Do not get drunk with wine, for that is debauchery, but be filled with the Spirit" (Ephesians 5:18).

You're How Old?

Many students who abuse alcohol are old enough to drink. The use and abuse of alcohol by underage students adds further complications. As you may know, the Lord established governments in order to create law and protect His people. We are to obey the government, as long as their directives do not contradict what God commands.

Most state governments have established age 21 as the legal age to purchase and consume alcohol. Despite this restriction, thousands of underage students drink. I witnessed this one fall semester not long ago when the Charleston police raided a hole-in-the-wall pizza joint with a bar in the basement. Eighty-six people were arrested for using fake identification. In many cases, it is easiest to drink underage at house parties or small gatherings, but for $60 to $80, you can get a fake ID in order to enjoy the bar scene.

The "High" Life

Besides the alcohol consumed at most college parties, there is an additional temptation—drugs. Marijuana is the most commonly used drug, but you will also run into folks who choose highly addictive drugs such as heroin, cocaine, and methamphetamines. Occasionally, you see folks using less popular drugs such as ecstasy and acid.

Other Dangers

Besides the obvious dangers and consequences associated with drinking and partying, there are some less noticed outcomes. One of the primary concerns is the effect on your school performance. Your primary task at college is to get an education. People who list socializing and partying as their top priority are throwing away tens of thousands of dollars. Considering going out on a weekday? Think twice—you don't want to oversleep and miss your chemistry lab. Common sense needs to come into play. You can't party the night away right before you have to finish a term paper or study for a midterm.

Still feeling tempted? Think again. Professors are generally not very compassionate. They seem to know who was out the night before, and they rarely relax their standards to accommodate your lack of preparation.

There is an even darker possibility for those who choose to party—date rape. It does and can happen, even for guys. If you choose to drink, watch your cup, your friends, and yourself. Never set your cup down, leave it unattended, or give it to someone else to watch, even if that means taking your cup into the bathroom with you. Don't let strangers give you a drink. You never know who might slip a date-rape drug such as Rohypnol, commonly known as a roofie, into it.

A male friend of mine was once at a college house party and was getting ready to leave. He set his cup down for only a second to put on his jacket. He grabbed the cup and was finishing the contents when someone yelled, "No! Don't drink that! You should probably go home now."

It was too late; he had already finished the drink. He does not remember how he made it home or what happened the rest of the night, for that matter. His roommate told him he was in the shower crying and vomiting for a several hours. To this day he does not know who drugged his drink and if it was meant for him or for someone else. What I do know is that I am grateful his story did not have a more tragic ending and that a female student did not finish the drink. What awful emotional and physical repercussions that girl could have experienced!

A good reputation is a great asset. Once it is tarnished with the abuse of alcohol and excessive partying, it can be hard to rebuild. The popularity of technology and social networking sites has only increased the problem. Those photos from last week's toga party just might end up on your friend's Facebook page tagged so that no one has to guess your identity. Add in the possible inappropriate comments to your wall post on Twitter or MySpace for the whole world to see, including professors and possible future employers. It helps to keep the "Grandma Rule" in mind when social networking. If you would be ashamed to have your grandmother see the things on your profile, then it is better not to have it up there. Better yet, keep the "Jesus Rule" in mind. Would you be ashamed if your Savior saw the same things? Too late; He already has (1 John 1:9). The good news is that He forgives us freely—I can't say the same for your grandma.

|||||||||||||||||||||||||||||

Have a Plan

The best way to avoid the various scary scenarios we've talked about in this chapter is not to put yourself in them in the first place. If, however, you feel a need to be part of the party scene, make sure you have a plan and stick to it.

- ○ First of all, know your limits and stay within them. You are responsible for yourself.

- ○ Use the buddy system, girls especially, and stick to it. It works well as long as you each hold up your end of the deal. Don't let the other person out of sight.

- ○ Have a designated driver or even a designated walker as an extra lookout. If you are that person, don't drink! Others are counting on you.

- ○ If you drink, stay away from excess. Shots, drinking games, and beer bongs quickly raise your blood-alcohol level to dangerous levels.

- ○ A good rule of thumb is to limit yourself to one drink an hour. Sipping a glass of water between alcoholic drinks will help moderate the effects.

- If things start moving or get blurry and you feel warm, stop. Cut yourself off because you don't want to go too far. It is never fun to spend a whole night with your head in the toilet or to have a hangover the next day.

It takes only one bad choice for your life to completely change. I once interviewed a campus police officer for an article on self-defense I was writing for the school newspaper. He said his biggest concern was for the countless number of girls he saw walking or staggering home by themselves in the wee hours of the morning. Don't let one evening of reckless fun destroy a lifetime of opportunities.

It's also possible to enjoy the social scene at parties without losing control of the situation—choose not to drink alcohol. There are all kinds of creative possibilities in this situation; some friends shared their favorites:

- At the beginning of the evening, get one beer from the keg and carry it around. This way, others won't hassle you about not having a drink. To make it look more realistic, I slowly pour out the contents as the evening wears on.

- Carry around a cup of your favorite soda or juice instead of alcohol.

If you choose not to drink at parties, some people may ask you why. I encourage you not to back down or shy away from the question. This is a wonderful opportunity to simply explain why you choose not to drink.

- If someone hassles you for not drinking, you might say that you are underage and that you respect the government and law God has ordained over us.

○ If you are of age and are asked why you don't drink excessively or partake in the drinking games, you can say you choose not to abuse the body God has given you.

The Bible tells us in 1 Corinthians 6:19 that our bodies are temples of the Holy Spirit within us and are from God. Moderation and caution will help us to refrain from abusing the bodies He has given to us. In everything, I encourage you to answer boldly for your faith and your actions. Remember to answer boldly, but don't be preachy. Respond confidently, but humbly, to be the most effective witness for your Savior.

A Positive Place

As a Christian, you can still have a good time on campus. Just remember who you are or, more important, *whose* you are!

In 1 Peter 2:9, the apostle Peter reminds us, "You are a chosen race, a royal priesthood, a holy nation, a people for His own possession, that you may proclaim the excellencies of Him who called you out of darkness into His marvelous light." God called each one of us out of sin to be His chosen and holy people. What an honor! Always remember who you are and for whom you live. It will keep things in perspective when tempted to abuse the gifts God has given us, including alcohol and time to hang out with friends.

You can have a good time on campus without resorting to the means some think is necessary to have a good time. There are plenty of fun things to do without drinking. Fun is what you make of it.

Getting involved with a Christian campus ministry through a local church near campus or a ministry center on campus is a wonderful way to stay plugged in to God's Word and enjoy Christian fellowship and encouragement to live a life for Christ. Your faith can be strengthened through Bible studies, worship opportunities, and the fellowship that comes with it. Seeing fellow Christians on campus and building these friendships is another wonderful way to be encouraged and to encourage others.

Campus ministries offer a great way to make new friends too. Having a core group of solid Christian college friends is priceless. I know it is for me. They offer a source of encouragement and stability. We hold each other accountable to stay committed to our faith and Christian living. They act as my family away from home.

Finally, there are innumerous ways to entertain yourself without partying or drinking. There is more to do than watching movies or playing video games. Get together and hold fun theme nights. You could hold cook-offs using only the dorm microwaves. Do music-swaps or game nights.

Extracurricular activities are also a great way to get involved and to keep temptation at bay. Intramural sports, clubs, organizations, and volunteer opportunities abound on campuses to help you get involved and stayed connected to the campus and to supportive people.

When I first drove into Collegetown, USA, I wasn't sure what Eastern Illinois University would hold for me. I found a wonderful group of Christian friends through the Lutheran campus ministry who encourage me and strengthen me in my desire to live in a Christlike way. I serve as a peer leader with this campus ministry organization and on the staff of the college yearbook. These activities help me to stay focused on why I am at college.

So while you are experiencing your first few weeks at college and enjoying your first taste of complete independence, remember you are still God's child, part of His holy priesthood, His witnesses in this world. "Blessed is the man who remains steadfast under trial, for when he has stood the test he will receive the crown of life, which God has promised to those who love Him" (James 1:12).

 C.K.

Self-Preservation

> *"Therefore* do not throw away your confidence, which has a great reward. For you have need of endurance, so that when you have done the will of God you may receive what is promised." Hebrews 10:35–36

Emotional and Social Health

Success in college, and ultimately in life, will take more consideration than simply making sure all assignments are turned in on time. It is extremely important to be sure to address your own personal needs as well, and to ensure that your attitude and health are in a positive condition. Too much of anything can be harmful, and this applies to both study and play. Study too much, and you risk becoming a brilliant hermit. Play too much, and you gamble becoming a sleep-deprived automaton running around the hallway in nothing but a bathrobe and foam football-mascot hat.

|||||||||||||||||||||||||||||

Time Management

One of the easiest traps to fall into is abuse of time management. College kids have struggled with this balance for years, even before the invention of time-sucking video games and networking sites (beware of these; they defy the space-time continuum). The equilibrium between finding time to study, play, and socialize is delicate but not unattainable. One of the easiest methods to achieve this goal is also the simplest—design a schedule for your day, and then follow it.

Taking things as they come can be fun, exciting, and decidedly bohemian, but it can also throw a routine or goal completely askew. Instead, develop a chart (by hand or computer, whichever appeals to you) and define basic time periods every day. Block out the intervals for your classes, and see what time you have left over with those key elements removed. If you have a part-time job, factor in the amount of time you work. Remember to plan for meals, personal hygiene, and sleep. Whatever white space on the chart is left glaring at you after you've determined the basic necessities can be filled by studying, hanging out with friends, or blowing bubbles. That's one of the glories of college—it's your call.

When you do set aside time to study, make sure that it is time *fully* dedicated to study. You are there to learn, and the responsibility of keeping yourself accountable is no one's but your own. Stay away from and off of engrossing Web sites, and unless television aids your concentration, keep it turned off. The same applies to music—if it is a distraction, eliminate it. If not, plug in your CD or MP3 player and have at the homework. If you find that you need to get away from a roommate or stuffy dorm room to study effectively, find a comfy tree trunk, library desk, or chemistry table. Be as fully committed to your work as it is possible to be. Unless you have a keen ability to multitask, dividing your attention between several things will usually lead to more time being spent on the completion of one activity than planned.

Homework can be boring at first (especially if you happen to be studying a wonderful subject like Latin), but the more quickly you accustom yourself to *actively* studying, the easier it will become, and the ability to study well will be critical to the rest of your time in college.

Once the work is done, feel free to move on to whatever the next item on your time schedule may be. Include some time every week, if not every day, to relax and hang out with friends. Play Frisbee, kickball, chess, or even tiddlywinks, but be sure to get in some play. It does not have to be conventional play: some of the most fun I ever had on campus involved spinning around on the campus green at 3:00 a.m. with a good friend until we fell over from dizziness. Before that, we pretended to be performers and put on a half-hour imaginary dance performance that somehow combined hip-hop and martial arts. You can do fun, juvenile things like that—it is allowed!

Games, especially those involving physical exercise, are natural stimulants for your body to produce positive endorphins. Endorphins are natural pain relievers that also promote a sense of well-being, a perfect follow-up to stress from studying. Endorphins also help get you in a better mood so that you can enjoy more of life. Even a walk on your own is better than staying inside with the blinds closed. And believe it or not, endorphins also help you burn up calories faster, which equals losing weight. So, in effect, you can keep yourself fit just by playing tag.

In the event that you have not made any friends yet or simply do not own a Frisbee, look into campus-sponsored events. Most colleges have on-campus entertainment that they advertise on everything that does not move, from newspaper ads to flyers handed out near the dining facilities. Florida State University, for example, has a movie theater, bowling alley, Paint-a-Pot, and a safe hangout called Club Downunder. Ask someone who looks bored to come join you for a game of bowling or a walk to the gym. At the very best, you will have gained a new friend; at the very worst, you will have an interesting story to tell.

Manage your time well, and you'll not only be successful but you will also have a blast doing it. What is there to resist in a deal like that?

Keep Connected

It is easy to become intoxicated by college. There is complete freedom of choice. You do not have to report or answer to anyone except yourself and your personal standards. Conversely, it can be intimidating to assume so much responsibility in such a short time. Whether you never want to go home again or whether going home is all you can think about, it is important to maintain a connection to home.

Regardless of what you may be doing or how many papers you may be working on, keep your parents and/or relatives informed of what you are doing in school and how things are working out for you. They care about you and about your success, and if you shut them out of your college experience, whether intentionally or accidentally, you risk creating a rift that may be difficult to heal. Remember: you are the one changing the living arrangements. Take the responsibility to discuss reasonable times and modes of contact before you leave home. This can help avoid parental fears, awkward moments, and helicopter parents. Then honor those guidelines to establish trust and support. Call your parents at least once every week, if not more frequently, to check in and let them know how you are. Write a letter to your grandparents or start up a Web blog where relatives can check in and see all your new adventures (or at least some of them).

In addition to calls and letters, arrange for home visits every so often. There are few things stronger than family ties, and being close to the ones you love for holidays or occasional weekends will boost your spirits as well as strengthen the bond between you and your family. Leaving home for good will take place in about four years or so, and that will be more dramatic than it needs to be if you do not get your parents used to the idea of you living out of the house. Guaranteed, they will have as rough a time of it as you will. Start the habit of keeping up communication early. Then the separation will be easier and you will continue to have a family support system in place even though you may not be living under the same roof.

||||||||||||||||||||||||||||||

Anti-Stagnation

It takes a good amount of courage to do something new and different, especially if you run the risk of doing something stupid in front of the infamous college peer group. Those who do not take the initiative to go out and make friends or explore new spots on campus are usually the ones with few, if any, good friends and no fun in their lives whatsoever. It is easy to get caught up in a comfortable, nonrisky routine. Do not let this happen to you.

The easiest solution to breaking the boredom of a day-to-day routine is to get out and explore the many hidden secrets that college has to offer. Let us pretend that you are a law major, but you love theater, music, and shows. There could be a huge group of potential friends to be made in the theater club or band hangout spot—but you'll never know, because you have never checked out anything not relating to your major. Besides, it would just be awkward for you to randomly show up, right? Never mind that college is the perfect place to be random and try new things. It is just not worth the chance, so you never go.

Hear that sound? That was opportunity throwing together a suitcase and slamming the door in frustration while hollering something about seeing you in court.

Check out college club meetings that you normally would not seek out. Make a game of it—try to go to at least one different club meeting per week. You may discover something that you did not know existed, and you might really like it (and the people there)!

Going hand-in-hand with the practice of meeting new people is the determination to consciously try new things. Even if it is as small as trying the unidentifiable meat in the dining hall, do something that makes every day a new experience. Your mind thrives off of new information and ideas, and you will find that by taking the initiative to try new things, you actually enhance your quality of life and mental attitude.

An adage says, "Variety is the spice of life." It is quite true, but like all spices, you have to figure out for yourself which kinds you are willing to try.

Physical Health

At most colleges, there is a myth, usually along the lines of the "Freshman Fifteen," that refers to the amount of weight freshmen are said to gain in college. As fun as it is to joke about the situation, it is a sad truth that your physical health is more likely to decline at college than at home. The good news is that there are numerous steps you can take to make sure that you'll be able to fit into your favorite jeans or T-shirt at the end of the year.

Eat Right

Pop-Tarts may be the food of choice for dorms in an ideal world, but the calorie and sugar counts in those little piece-of-heaven-pastries will quickly put on the pounds. Steer away from heavier snacks, like the aforementioned Pop-Tarts or pastries and chocolate stashes. Stock up instead on healthier snacks that take a longer time to eat, such as popcorn or nuts. Many students tend to eat when they're bored. Try to avoid this trap by staying involved in something, whether it is homework or volunteering.

There is also the common misconception that if you skip meals or fast, you will lose weight more quickly. This is not true. If you do not eat for long amounts of time, you will likely eat too much the next time you have a decent meal, and you will be more likely to indulge in several high-sugar treats to try to regulate your dropping blood-sugar levels.

A better method is to eat three square meals a day and be smart about it. Choose healthy foods, and if you absolutely must, try eating about half of what you normally do at meals with some snacks scattered throughout the day to keep you from crashing. Healthy food choices include fruits and vegetables, nuts, meat/protein, and fish. Instead of drinking heavily sugared sodas, try water, tea, or coffee.

Sleep and Fitness

Eating right will not, on its own, keep you healthy and happy. It is a great idea to marry that strategy with good fitness practices and plenty of sleep.

Again, most colleges have a gym or track that you can use. Thirty minutes of exercise a day for three days of the week will do wonders for your metabolism, helping you digest food and burn off fat and calories. In addition, physical exercise helps your mood, since exercise gets more oxygen into your bloodstream, which makes you feel better.

If weights and running are not for you, try something more low-key like yoga or Pilates. The great thing about these types of exercise is that they can be done in your dorm room—no getting up early to hike to the gym! Yoga in particular is beneficial because of its wide range of application—there are poses to address specific therapeutic areas, and the mental focus required helps to de-stress and promote better concentration. Pilates develops strength, muscle endurance, and flexibility. Even as few as fifteen minutes of either routine every morning can help boost your metabolism (so that you use energy more effectively) and increase your muscle strength and stamina.

Walking is a great opportunity on college campuses, especially since you will likely do much of it just on your way to classes! Try walking a bit faster than you normally do, and make sure that your posture is upright and correct—this helps you get the most exercise out of a walk. Playing is another great way to get into shape while having fun at the same time. If you are on a sports team, there is a lot of camaraderie to be found in addition to the exercise. If you are not much of an athlete, get together some friends for a game of tag or lawn baseball. If it is absolutely sweltering outside, challenge friends to participate in active indoor games.

After a long day, resist the urge to stay up until two in the morning. Sleep is chronically underappreciated—everyone wants more of it, but no one wants to give up late-night "chilling" time. Get yourself out of this habit, and get yourself to bed in time to get at least seven to eight hours of sleep a night. You will be more rested and alert the next day, which will promote a more productive and enjoyable experience in class and with your friends. While in college, you also possess the choice of whether to take a nap or not (they're not just for kindergartners anymore!). Should you have to cut out on sleep for a few nights, a midday nap helps you recharge and boost your ability to get through the rest of the day without passing out from exhaustion.

If you take the steps now to make yourself healthy (and therein more likely successful), you will reap the reward of living a longer, more enjoyable life. By exercising thirty minutes every day, you can lower blood pressure, strengthen your heart and cardiovascular system, maintain a healthy body weight, reduce stress, and increase your muscle tone and strength. There is nothing to lose and everything to gain—so go hit the gym every few days!

|||||||||||||||||||||||||||||

Health at School

Making sure that you take care of yourself does not necessarily mean that everyone else will do the same. On a college campus, especially a crowded one, colds and diseases spread like a well-fueled fire. There is no way to guard against *everything*, no matter how many times you sanitize your hands.

That said, it would be wise to assemble a basic health supply set. You should include the standard items such as headache and anti-inflammatory treatments, along with a first-aid kit. Bring hand sanitizer and cleaning supplies. Dorm rooms, especially bathrooms, can quickly become breeding grounds for mold and bacteria. By taking the steps to keep your space clean, you can increase the chance that you won't be lying in bed with a throbbing headache and fever.

In the event that a headache or fever does crop up, do not be a martyr. If you cannot take care of it yourself, go to the student health center. At the beginning of the year, make a trip to the health center. Orient yourself with the procedures there so that you know what you need to do if you ever need to sign yourself in. All college health centers ask for insurance papers and health records so they can have your information on file and available if needed. Make sure you have all that paperwork (including immunization records, contact numbers, and eye prescriptions, if applicable) turned in prior to the beginning of the school year—hopefully you will never need it, but if you do, it will be readily located in their file cabinet and not lodged in a lump under your bed.

Do not ever feel ashamed or embarrassed to go to the health center. There are a lot of kids who feel like it could be an invasive visit, with awkward questions and embarrassing phone calls. No matter what is going on, whether it is drugs, pregnancy, STDs, or a simple head cold, you do not have to deal with it alone. The health center is a wonderful resource as long as you are not too intimidated to get there.

Drugs and Social "Fun"

First and foremost, remember that you are a beloved child of God. There is nothing you can possibly do that would make Him stop loving you. This does not, however, mean that you can do what you like and deny that you have done anything wrong. If you do something that you have second thoughts about, or that you feel was wrong, talk to someone at your church or at a guidance office. Talk to God. He listens and forgives. "If we confess our sins, He is faithful and just to forgive us our sins and to cleanse us from all unrighteousness. If we say we have not sinned, we make Him a liar, and His Word is not in us" (1 John 1:9–10).

Parties can be a great way to get out, meet people, and make friends. They are not for everyone, and it is true that they are a popular hot spot for drug deals, drugged alcoholic beverages, and smoking chains. If you are going to go to a party, be smart about it. A good rule of thumb is to not drink anything that you have not been *constantly* watching, from the moment the soda can was opened to the present instant that it is in your hand. Go with a friend to help each other stay safe.

Regarding alcohol: remember that if you decide to drink heavily, you will probably end up with a hangover. Hangovers are not the greatest experience on the planet. Your head feels like it is splitting open, the smallest sound is grating, and your roommate will probably end up either bringing you a trash can or leading you into the bathroom to hurl (it depends on the kindness and time availability of your roomie). It is easy to be caught up in the moment of the party, but before you accept anything in a red cup, you need to decide for yourself whether it is worth the worship of a porcelain god in the morning. Of course, all of this is in addition to the legal ramifications of underage drinking and collegiate consequences.

Drugs—no matter what people may tell you about the false alarms on health or the "sweet" high you may get from them—are bad. It is as simple as that. In addition to damaging your internal organs and/or brain cells, and leading you to do stupid and potentially life-threatening feats under their influence, they're highly addictive and *very* expensive. Not to mention illegal—your one call from jail is not a good way to fulfill your required weekly call home.

One new textbook is about the same price as two rows of cocaine, and that's if you're getting the stuff from a friend who cuts you a deal on the price. It can easily add up to a semester's worth of fees for a week's worth of highs. If you begin doing drugs regularly, it is an absolute guarantee that your student debt will be *much* larger than it would be from the tuition alone. Many students, to support their drug habits, cut classes to do part-time work in order to get more money. Others dip into their scholarship funds. Either way, it is illegal, damaging, and not conducive to your success. Did we discuss illegal?

Drugs are also dangerous in that the more you use them, the higher a tolerance to them you develop. When your tolerance to the drug rises, so does the amount that you will have to take in order to get the same high that you did previously. Take enough of the drug, and you will overwhelm your system, which can possibly result in death.

Marijuana is the most commonly abused drug, probably because it is one of the easiest to access. After an initial high, users will probably experience feelings of depression, sleepiness, anxiety, or fear. Ultimately, marijuana destroys your ability to pay attention, to remember facts or people, and to learn. To put it bluntly, it is the best way to destroy your chances of succeeding in college.

Heroin, in particular, is highly addictive. Use it long enough, and you will collapse your veins, infect the lining of your heart and heart valves, and provoke liver disease. Withdrawal from the drug, usually after a few hours, includes muscle and bone pain, uncontrollable diarrhea and vomiting, restlessness, and insomnia. Unless your dream occupation involves a criminal record, steer clear.

Feel free to conduct some of your own research on drugs and their effects. Some students will question your refusal, or ask why it is "so bad" to do drugs. Most students are eventually swayed to try drugs because they honestly do not know or cannot think of the risks that accompany individual drugs. Know the consequences, and convince *yourself* otherwise—who better to trust? Your statement of the facts may help your friend realize the risk that they are taking. Lead by example!

A certain kind of recreational smoking, called hookah, has begun climbing in popularity over the past few years, especially with regard to the college scene. While it does not have the same effect as cigarettes or other tobacco-based products (it tastes like flavored smoke), it releases carbon monoxide into your system. There is some carbon monoxide already in your body, but the levels that a hookah session will raise it to will begin killing off brain cells. As you may or may not know, brain cells do not grow back. You have a fixed amount of them when you are born, and that is the amount that you are left to work with through the remainder of your life. Hookah is not illegal, but smoke too much of it, and you will rival the caterpillar from *Alice in Wonderland* at spouting nonsense. Best leave the puffing to book characters.

||||||||||||||||||||||||||||

Spirit and Mind

The fact that you have moved away from your home church is no excuse for letting your faith stagger along behind your studies. Most campuses (or nearby areas) have churches of almost every denomination. Many campuses or campus towns include a Lutheran church.

Join a church on campus. Keep in mind that "join" here does not mean "Go to Sunday service and disappear for the rest of the week." "Join" means to actively plug yourself into the spiritual community and take a front seat in helping with service projects, planning retreats, or even holding the door open on Sunday morning. There are limitless opportunities to be found if you take the initiative to look for them. Serving others, in addition to being Christ's direction for us, is immensely fulfilling and often fun. You'll learn more about this in other chapters of this book.

Another way to expand your horizons and service hour count is to join a club or a discussion group. Colleges may as well be called Club Capitals—most host over one hundred clubs on their campus, while major universities may have four hundred or more. Chances are good that you can find at least one in which you are interested. If you are more interested in evolving opinion or obtaining a wider scope of things, look into a discussion group.

Discussion groups are great ways to meet people, and they get you accustomed to speaking in groups, which is an important life skill to obtain. The earlier you begin practicing how to present your ideas in a group, the better. An added bonus is that most discussion groups are a low-key format—if you happen to stutter, you will not lose a client or a job because of it.

It all comes down to making sure you keep up the connections that you have and also work to make new ones. The more genuine love and care that you have in your life, the happier and more motivated you will be.

Taking care of yourself means taking care of *every* part of yourself—emotional, physical, and spiritual. Keep yourself happy and healthy, pray when you may not be as happy or healthy as you would like to be, and the rest of a wonderful first year will follow from there.

 L.F.

seven

Finances:
The Big Green
Monster

If you are planning on going straight to bed after reading this chapter, do not. If you have any concern for your own well-being, you will best be served by simply putting this book down and not picking it back up until after a hearty meal. A full stomach is the least you can do for yourself when beginning to discuss money in college.

Most people will approach financial independence in one of two ways. Some simply choose to ignore it for as long as possible (generally the entirety of college) under the good graces of parental guidance. Others play the "deer in the headlights" role, freezing, panicking, and being violently run over by an eighteen-wheel bank statement. While one of these options may seem infinitely more attractive than the other, the fact is that neither is particularly effective. Like so many other facets of your college experience, you'll find that managing your money will be a chance to prove your independence while still accepting guidance from other, more qualified individuals.

The Expected

||||||||||||||||||||||||||||

Tuition

Consider this story of three little pigs. Together these three pigs frolicked through the halls of a coastal Florida high school, completing service projects, partaking in extra-curricular activities, and studying ever so diligently for their standardized tests. The first little piggy came from a pretty standard middle-income family. He was smart, but not quite as hardworking as the other two piggies. He knew he wanted to receive a post-secondary education, but he was unsure what he wanted to do with it. Without any particular course laid out for him, and without any gratuitous amounts of disposable income, the first little piggy graduated from high school and decided to stay in town and attend a community college and find his life's calling.

The second little piggy came from a similar financial bracket as the first piggy. Her family wasn't so good with money, but they always seemed to have enough to provide for their piglets. But this little piggy had higher ambitions. She wanted to go to nursing school and possibly spend a few years traveling the world with the Peace Corps. She had done some research and realized her test scores and overall GPA were strong enough to get her into a four-year public college. She applied to the state school four hours away, where she was eventually accepted on reduced tuition because of her status as an in-state student.

The third little piggy wanted to leave it all behind. Like the first two piggies, she didn't come from the richest of litters, so she was often faced with questions of how she could possibly afford a school so far away. For four years, she worked as hard as possible, organizing events and volunteering with the bird sanctuary until she was finally accepted to NYU. Though the third little piggy was jumping for joy at the sight of her acceptance letter, the thought of having to pay for school finally settled in, and she was much more afraid than she had ever imagined.

Many of your long-term college choices will be made for you before you even arrive. In fact, when choosing a school, it is often the cost of tuition that will be the overriding factor in your decision. Though tuition is easily the largest expense of almost any college student, it is something that is easy to plan and prepare for.

There are three basic types of colleges or universities; all three have very different financial expectations for their students. The largest universities tend to be four-year public schools—the University of (*insert state here*) or (*any of the fifty United States*) University. These schools often offer reduced tuition for students already living in that state. However, even out-of-state students find it cheaper to attend a public school in another state than to attend most private schools.

Private schools are easily the most attractive to students, which leads to their being easily the most expensive.

✳ College Economics 101: Supply and Demand

If you have fifteen bags of ramen noodles, and thirty of your friends would like one of those bags, you can charge more for them. However, if you have the same fifteen bags of ramen noodles and only five friends who want to buy them, you can charge only a fraction of the price than if you had more friends. Lesson: More friends means more money!

Don't be fooled—private schools do offer many benefits beyond just prestige (one-of-a-kind professors, a more close-knit community, better cafeteria food), but these are the kinds of things that potential students need to put a price tag on. Some people are willing to pay large amounts of money to sleep in the same dorm as the guy from *Law and Order*'s daughter and to listen to lectures from the foremost author in ant studies. Private schools can offer a vast range of benefits, but let's face it, not everyone can afford $45,000 a year.

Local and more affordable, community college has become more and more attractive in recent years. Many community colleges even offer online degree programs so that virtually anybody can receive a college degree without the added expenses of travel and housing. Community college can also be a good place to decide what it is you are looking for in your college education. A two-year/two-year plan consists of two years at a community college and then two years at a larger school. That way, if you decide after two years of studying applied physics that you would like to go straight into the workforce training dogs for a living, those two years won't have been that expensive.

Books

This is the cheapest book you will buy for college. The first time you go to buy books it will, unequivocally, be the most depressing act of your week. If you never thought you could spend more on books in a day than you could on groceries for a month, you didn't think hard enough. But again, like your tuition, the cost of books is something you can plan for in advance. Your most expensive books will be textbooks, the large, hardback books with cheesy collages on the front.

Math classes, science class, business classes—all of these types of courses could run you well over $300 in book fees. Ironically enough, the cheapest books you will buy will be for more advanced English courses. Barring anthologies, reading a paperback novel will not cost you a quarter of what a financial accounting book will.

Most colleges want you to buy your books directly from the school bookstore. Shop for books the same way you would a pair of jeans. Look around! Online book giants such as Amazon.com sometimes offer $45 textbooks for literally only a penny. Web sites such as ULoop.com allow students to trade books (and virtually anything else you could imagine) without going back through the bookstore.

✱ Tip: Beating the System!

It is actually possible to make money on books. Don't be afraid to buy your books online and then sell them back to the bookstore. Every college bookstore offers a buyback period at the end of the year, where they will offer you cash for your books. If you can find a book for cheap online and then sell it back to the bookstore for more than you bought it for, you just bought yourself an extra Homewrecker at Moe's.

Housing

For as much as college is supposed to be like the "real world," there are very few times in life when you will have to pay just to be there. That is, of course, unless you decide to join the ever-elusive Sam's Club. However, there is one expense that is definitive of not only the college experience but also of a real-world experience. Depending on the institution, housing can easily become even more expensive than tuition. And although there aren't many ways to avoid paying for housing, there is a way to determine how to get the biggest bang for your buck. Let's examine.

A freshman in college really has only two options when it comes to housing, either living on campus or off campus. While, financially speaking, one of these options probably makes a lot more sense than the other, this is not a decision you want to make based solely on money. At many schools, two semesters of living in a dorm will cost roughly the same as one year in a standard student-housing apartment complex. However, many schools require students who live in certain dorms to purchase a ridiculously over-priced meal plan. Don't get me wrong—free access to an all-you-can-eat buffet seems like heaven, but the nutritional value of a pizza and Rice-Krispies-treat diet is somewhat lacking.

Living in a dorm for a year is a very good idea. In terms of the convenience, the proximity to new people, and the chance to build a surprisingly high tolerance for bad roommate habits, there is nothing quite like a dorm room. Some of those experiences you can't put a price on. But for some people, sharing all but ten square feet of your space is simply not an option. For those people, off-campus housing is readily available. And, to be frank, it is often the more financially responsible decision.

Let's face it—there is something very adult sounding about living in an apartment. Not only does it mean an environment where the only authority is a landlord but it also means a lot more personal accountability. *Insert crashing thunder here!* Yes, personal accountability for you! Finances can get significantly more difficult when moving into an apartment, but it can also be a good chance to practice good fiscal habits. Here's a quick list of things an apartment renter might have to be responsible for that a dorm resident may not.

- Utility bills (electricity, water, sewage)

- Cable/Internet

- Pots, pans, dishes, utensils

- Groceries

- Trash bags

- An actual vacuum cleaner

- Sponges, dish soap, washcloths

- Light bulbs

- Toilet paper

- And, if you intend on retaining your sanity, some sort of wall décor

Essentially, an apartment will allow twelve months of living for about the equivalent of nine months in a dorm room. It's easy to allow your extraneous expenses to pile up, but, again, part of the apartment experience is practicing personal accountability. *Insert more crashing thunder!* Deciding among your housing options is simply something that will require more than a budgeting strategy. Weigh all the options.

The Unexpected

It was a Saturday morning, and Davey was taking a leisurely jog around his neighborhood. After about twenty minutes of steady exercise, Davey was hit over the head with a dead fish from the sky, sending him violently to the ground.

Unfortunately, there was no way for Davey to foresee a fish falling on him that Saturday morning. And this is a fact of life—there are certain things for which we cannot prepare. It seems counterintuitive for a section on dealing with the unexpected to even exist. There are, however, many college expenses that are easy to overlook, sometimes to the point of extreme detriment.

Are you driving a car right now? flying in a plane? commanding a horse-drawn chariot? If this is the case, then you are certainly aware of the value of transportation. Getting to and from school can often be more stressful than the schoolwork itself. With fewer and fewer airlines flying cross-country, finding a flight to fit your specifications, let alone one within your price range, is a taxing process. It is, however, impossible to ignore the dilemma of travel, whether it is to and from school or around school itself.

Consider this: Two students from the same city in Georgia decide to go to two different schools. Benny wants to be an architect, so Georgia Tech, only an hour away, seems like a perfect fit. June, however, doesn't care for construction or design. June wants to be an actress, and she, like any high school student with acting ambition, knows that the only place to be a true actress is New York City. A month before move-in, Benny begins to pack his knickknacks, things he knows he won't need to use between now and then, but things he would still very much like to have at school with him: his gumball machine, his complete set of original Star Wars character bobble heads.

At the same time, June is in the process of finding a plane ticket to Newark International. She can pack only two fifty-pound bags according to the airline, but she knows she still has to get herself and her bags from Jersey to Manhattan. It will cost June $240 to fly to the Newark, $50 in cab fare to get into the city, and $130 to ship the rest of her luggage. For Benny, it will cost $15 in gas. This is not to say that either of these options is unreasonable, but when traveling greater distances, the costs can certainly pile up.

Most state universities are notoriously large. The University of Tennessee enrolls roughly 26,000 students a year. Florida State University enrolls some 41,000. These numbers seem simply unreal. That is, *until* it comes time to find a parking space. An often-overlooked expense that comes accompanied by a handful of other minor expenses is the gift and the curse of owning a car at school. Many schools charge students a one-time fee to park their cars on campus. This can be several hundred dollars. On top of a campus-parking pass, if you choose to live in an apartment complex, you may also have to pay to park there. Essentially, your car is forced to pay tuition just like you. But a parking pass can't pay for itself like an education.

Assuming that you intend to drive your car and not simply use it as an ornament for the nearest parking lot, remember to consider the cost of movement. While gas is an obvious expenditure, natural wear and tear can sneak up at the most inconvenient of times. The worst-case scenario would have you in a city you don't know very well and the car's ignition system cuts out or the battery dies with nobody around. Vehicle maintenance can cost a pretty penny, so it is better to take preventative measures than to deal with it after a problem occurs.

* Tip: Vacationing

One of the sweetest things about college is the fact that you now have friends living in different cities all across the country. Take advantage of their floors and couches! A weekend away for only the cost of gas or a plane ticket can be a lot of fun. You may even be able to pay for your food with the change you find between their cushions.

Cyndi Lauper was a prophet, the most terrible, terrible, terrible kind of prophet. Girls do just want to have fun. I'm not suggesting that fun is a gender-biased activity, but there seems to be a certain point when girls decide they just want to have fun and boys decide they just want to make the girls happy doing whatever it takes. Whatever it takes usually involves spending money. Nobody has this image of going to college and sitting around in a dark room with the AC turned off for the sake of saving money. Spending money on entertainment isn't a bad thing. What can be fun is finding creative ways to avoid spending too much.

Idea 1: Gastronomically Adventurous. Whether it is dinner in a cafeteria or at a dining room table every night, over time, any eating habit can become mundane. The way to solve this usually implies a bag with a big yellow M on it. But one thing that remains true of almost any college town is that there will be dozens of kitschy, affordable, creative restaurants. A group of friends can easily form some sort of schedule to eat out once a month at a new restaurant. Sure, this may lead to a lot of sushi while people get comfortable with the idea, but sushi certainly beats a fish fillet with a side of fries.

Idea 2: Friday Night Talkies. Going to the movies is probably one of the easiest things to do on a night when there's not much else to do.

"Hey, Johnny," said Phil, "I've got a calc exam on Tuesday. Want to go see some people get their heads ripped off in the new Rob Zombie movie before I go into hibernation for the weekend?"

"Absolutely!" answered Johnny.

Over time, though, going to the movies can become very expensive, especially if you're an avid fan of Sno-Caps. Instead of going out to the movies, bring the movies in. A Blockbuster or Netflix membership can cost as much for one month of unlimited rentals as going to see one movie at the theater. And watching a movie at home gives you the freedom to talk, eat, or press pause while you take a break.

Idea 3: Anything That Glows in the Dark. College kids are still kids. Most of the people you meet will still love to run around outside, get dirty, and scrape their knees. A glow-in-the-dark Frisbee can be a cheap, long-lasting investment, not only for the sake of saving money on the weekends but also for the sake of meeting new people. Some other awesome glow-in-the-dark toys include footballs, water guns, or even shoes (can you say manhunt?). Don't be afraid to still be a little goofy, especially if it means saving a little cash.

This isn't to say that the only things that will cost are cars and entertainment. In fact, it's possible even to overlook your own health. Buying medicine can make you feel a whole new kind of pain. But, again, as much as there is to be paid for in college, it can become overwhelming to try to recognize all those possibilities.

|||||||||||||||||||||||||||

How to Deal

At this point in the chapter, you're probably curled up in a corner in tears because you have absolutely no idea where you are going to get all this money. You may be looking on eBay trying to find the going rate for a vestigial organ or maybe even a kidney. You may be considering the one-time purchase of a boat so you can smuggle exotic animals into the country and start your own zoo. One of the first options that goes through anyone's mind is attempting to become a backup dancer for an up-and-coming R&B artist. (*What*? That *isn't* what goes through your mind?) But, as we all soon find out, dancing is harder than it looks, and the Coast Guard has invested in some pretty fast boats themselves. While people will do some crazy things for money, there are also some simple, practical ways of offsetting the cost of a good education.

In terms of attractiveness, getting a job is probably the pug of all income options. Unfortunately, it is also the most viable of options. Getting a job is not only a consistent source of income but it also provides future résumé material. Even the most menial of jobs is still work experience, something that is attractive to all future employers. When Phil (our moviegoer and lover of severed heads from earlier in this chapter) decided he wanted to work for a movie studio, he figured the best place to start would be in a sort of secretarial role for the front desk. He never would have guessed that his job answering phones at an apartment complex for two years would make him an attractive candidate.

There are a few standard places where most students will go first to look for a job. The number one employer of students is actually the school itself. Whether it is in the cafeteria, the residence halls, the library, the post office, or the intramural sports complex, there are thousands of part-time, minimum-wage jobs that colleges offer specifically to their students. One of the nicest aspects of these jobs is that they cater to the schedule of a full-time student. Sure you may be sorting mail for five hours a day, four days a week. But that also means you can spend less time mooching rides off of your friends without the intent to pay them back for gas. How do you find these jobs? Almost every campus will have some sort of career center or employment advising office that can point you in the right direction of both on- and off-campus job offers. Most of the time you can even find these listings on the school's Web site.

Work-study programs are the golden ticket of on-campus employment. Work-study essentially means you are working for your school, generally in your field of study, for the purpose of offsetting the cost of your tuition. It's like wanting to be a race car driver but the only way you can get near a race car is to clean the tires for a nickel after every race. Work-study programs can be excellent résumé material because the work is usually relevant to whatever it is you want to do with your life.

But wouldn't it be easier if somebody just gave you all this money? Don't you just wish you could say, "Hey, I'm a really good person. My life hasn't been super easy. Can't you cut me some slack for once and give me fistfuls of free education?" Luckily, this is sort of the way college scholarships work. You will be hard-pressed to find a college student who hasn't at least applied for some form of scholarship, let alone received one. Some of these scholarships are ridiculously large, while others are only big enough to pay for your dinner one night—your date may still have to pay for his or her own.

If you intend on staying at an in-state public school or even a community college, many states have a merit-based scholarship system that can pay up to 100 percent of your tuition. The state of Florida, for example, offers the Bright Futures program through which students with high enough grades and a certain number of community service hours get a free ride to any state school. Some of these types of programs even toss in a book allowance of a couple hundred dollars. These are the kinds of scholarships that are relatively easy to get, since they're totally based on what you are already doing.

Planning on going to college out of state? Just looking for more money as it is? There are thousands, literally, thousands, of people and corporations looking to give money to young people. Web sites such as scholarships.com (sounds too easy, right?) can help filter out some awards that might be of interest to you. And don't think that these scholarships are offered only to high school seniors. Even college professors receive grants based on an application process.

A good rule of thumb is that the more difficult the application process for a scholarship, the more it will be worth it. If you have to write an essay, there is a solid chance that you've already eliminated three-quarters of the competition who refuse to sit down and write five hundred words about themselves. If you have to come up with some sort of project proposal, you're probably in even better shape. Ever had something absolutely terrible happen in your life? College is the perfect time to allow that adversity to earn you some money. It sounds a little self-serving, but there comes a point where one's personal struggles become something to be embraced and shared, especially if it means your dream school becomes a reality. College is a gift. The chance to become a more well-rounded individual with a clear direction toward benefiting society is not something that should be a financial disaster. Scholarships are meant to keep you out of debt and moving forward.

But, if all else fails, debt may not be the worst thing in the world. In fact, it can be sort of humbling. Financial aid (loan, Pell grant, etc.) is available, usually based on need. This is where the horror stories of student loans following someone to his grave begin. What's often overlooked is the fact that well more than half the people in college are receiving financial aid. FinAidFacts.com has available all sorts of great resources and information on financial aid. There, you can read that some 63 percent of students are enrolled in some sort of grant or loan program. Sure, there may be a big green monster chasing you for the next thirty years, but it is relatively comforting to know that you won't be the only one being chased. Over $44 million in financial aid is given out every year. Why shouldn't you be a part of that?

✱ Tip: Put Your Debt into Perspective

The most expensive schools in the country run somewhere around $50,000 a year for tuition plus housing and expenses. For four years, that's $200,000 in potential loans. How much does your potential career pay? If you plan on being a lawyer, doctor, computer analyst, or accountant, you should be in pretty good shape to pay those loans back quickly. If you plan on being an English teacher, experimental farmer, or rock wall enthusiast, you may want to prepare yourself for many, many years of payments.

Whatever the case may be, it is a good idea to try building some sort of safety net. A savings account with a few hundred dollars is always a good idea, just in case something drastic happens (car breaks down, salmonella outbreak puts you in the hospital, very tiny meteorite lands in your living room destroying the carpet). It's also a good idea to start building a relationship with your bank. It simply makes it easier when a strange financial situation arises to be in good standing with the people who watch over your money. And you can always earn a little bit of interest on the money you put away.

|||||||||||||||||||||||||

A Few Things to Consider

Obviously, college can be one of the most expensive endeavors of anyone's life. In fact, the only investments that may be more expensive are a house, a child, or a traveling show exhibiting invasive species of primates. If you plan on owning those things, you might need to find a book more tailored to the occasion. As far as school is concerned, learning how to and thinking about paying for the necessities can become a hobby in itself. And while financial know-how seems like something everyone would want to possess, focusing too hard on your money can be destructive.

As much as this chapter has focused on the little expenses that can sneak up on you, or the ways to save an extra twenty dollars by bending the system, there are certain expenses that remain totally in the control of the student. Tithing, for example, is something that logic would assume to be nonexistent in college, like vacuums or a well-cooked meal. When you are struggling for money, it can be difficult to give to something from which you don't get an immediate, tangible gratification. It's like putting money into one of those machines where the gumball spins through a surprisingly long, surprisingly entertaining spiral before reaching the bottom for you to grab. Only, instead of spinning through the tube, the machine just gives a note saying, "Thank you for your gift! Because of you, a gumball in Africa will be able to have a new coat of sugar painted on tomorrow."

Nothing can be a greater test of your faith than giving of yourself when you feel like you have nothing left to give.

To lay a trust in God so deep that you believe the five days worth of groceries you can afford will be able to last you fifty days is the most terrifying experiment in humility you may ever face. Giving to the church or to a charity or simply giving your time to a service group will not give you financial wealth, but it will certainly make you stronger in the face of one of our world's greatest dangers—poverty.

This isn't to say that every college student winds up homeless and without food for a couple of years before getting herself on her feet. In fact, it's almost the opposite. College is a strange microcosm of society. It isn't really the real world, but more like a portal to the real world, where you get to try most things, mess them up, and then learn how to do better the next time. It's the same way with money. Budgeting your finances is a great practice to start in college. It is not something you are going to get right on the first try. If you're having trouble working out the numbers from your financial aid, or you're not sure what is covered by your scholarship, universities have entire departments that exist solely for the purpose of making sure you don't go broke while enrolled. Talk to the financial aid department. Better yet, if you have money questions, talk to your financial accounting professor. Colleges don't exist just to teach you what's in a book. They exist to teach you how to be a well-rounded member of society. Your educational resources are boundless, whether you need to learn how to handle your money or you want to learn what it's like to live on a boat in Italy. (Yes, it is guaranteed that somebody at your college has lived on a boat in Italy.)

✳ Tip: Don't Become Consumed!

Just reading this chapter is probably taking more time than you should ever spend consistently thinking about money unless someone is paying you to do so. Focusing too hard on your finances will lead to some of the most excruciating emotional and physical pain you may ever feel. Yes, be smart about your money, but don't try to be perfect. Nobody is ever perfect with money.

The most important point to remember about your school is that it is still a business, a group of people trying to make money. They are the ones who invited you to go there. You simply expressed an interest. Don't allow the big bad wolf to come and blow down your time at school. It is a time when you are meant to enjoy yourself, and even more so to learn how to enjoy yourself. Have faith. If worse comes to worse, you can always sell a kidney on eBay (just kidding!).

 E.M.

Academics and Technology

If you are like most college students, virtually your entire college experience will center around academics and technology. Without the academics portion of the experience, there wouldn't be an experience to talk about. Between trying to decide what to do with your life, picking the right classes, and handling the coursework, you may begin to feel overwhelmed. On top of that, you need to take into account the amount of adjustment when it comes to online work and technology requirements that supplement your classes. All of these concerns are just minor roadblocks that you will be able to work through. You will journey through all of the challenges, sometimes with joys, sometimes with hardships, but you can make it through. You may feel lost at times, but there will always be one resource or another to help you; you just have to know how to access these resources. So go ahead—make the most out of your academic experience and don't lose hope!

IIIIIIIIIIIIIIIIIIIIIIIIIII

Your Major

By this point in your life, somebody has probably asked you, "What do you want to be when you grow up?" The time has finally come to get serious about this question. Many of you have made that decision, while others have no idea. For many, what you decide today may not be what you choose tomorrow. I see many of my friends struggling with this decision. We are young and inexperienced, yet we are deciding what to do for the rest of our lives. Are we ready for this much responsibility? How should I decide? What if I make the wrong decision?

When you don't know, gather information, seek advice, and pray continuously. In Jeremiah 29:11, our heavenly Father reminds us, "For I know the plans I have for you." It may seem like you have no idea as to what you want, but God has already worked it out. His plan included the fact that you will serve Him honorably in whatever you do. Some people think you can serve God only by becoming a church worker or missionary, but that is completely wrong. In all that you do, you can serve God through your vocation. His plan for you includes not only your future career but also all of the ways you serve others through your vocation as student, future spouse, future parent, son, daughter, accountant, building foreman, or so many others.

I realize it would be nice if God just told you how He wants you to serve. But that would make you an automaton, simply repeating preprogrammed information. The challenge lies in identifying the life's work God has planned for you. Romans 8:28 says, "We know that for those who love God all things work together for good, for those who are called according to His purpose." As our lives play out, we discover who we are in Christ; it's worth the wait.

Registration

Whether or not you have a declared major, you will still have to sign up for classes and meet your academic adviser. Sound scary? For some students, registration can be a nerve-racking experience. After all, not only will you be picking all of your classes for your first college term, but you will also begin forming connections with other students, faculty, and advisers. Registration makes quite an impression on many new people. Remember that as you begin your registration day. Hopefully, during this time, you can take advantage of the circumstances and show Christ's love to others, as John writes in his Gospel, "By this all people will know that you are My disciples, if you have love for one another" (13:35). So, even if you feel a bit nervous or if something goes wrong on registration day, remember that you have the opportunity to reflect your faith in Christ to those who are going through the registration process with you. Don't worry! Even if you make a mistake on registration day, there are always second chances. As schedules allow, there is usually room to go back and make changes.

Now your next question might be "How does this registration thing take place?" Most schools publish a schedule of the dates for registration. You sign up to attend one of these days through the registrar. Typically, attendance is mandatory unless other arrangements are made. Many parents attend registration with their son or daughter the first time. Schools offer parents special sessions about gathering pertinent information, such as financial aid papers. For the students, programs include meeting with the academic school and their adviser, registering for classes, getting their student IDs, taking placement tests, and meeting new and current students. You gain loads of insight on what student life is like during registration day as well; it is never too early to find ways to get involved!

Selecting Classes and Electives

There are many things to keep in mind when choosing your required and elective classes. "Will the professor be any good?" "How big will the class be?" "Should I sign up for course sessions with my friends?" These are just a few of the common questions running through the average student's mind. These are important things to consider when making your course selections. If you would ask students from a variety of colleges and universities throughout the country, they will tell you that they shared these same concerns. Once you get into the swing of things, however, it really isn't so bad, and you will soon become accustomed to the process.

When choosing courses, it is good to have done some research. Look through the available class times and days to create several versions of a schedule that will work for your needs. Then your adviser will know that you did your homework, and you will be allowed to make more decisions about your schedule than if you had not been prepared. Your adviser's purpose is not to do everything for you, but rather to provide guidance when needed; college is about gaining responsibility and making decisions on your own.

I attend a small, private university, so my perspective on class sizes is somewhat biased by my experiences. I am thankful that most of the time I have small classes, averaging about thirty students per class. I have friends who go to state schools that have several hundred students in their classes, yet they would want it no other way. When I chose which college to attend, I paid close attention to school and class size. I liked the thought that at a smaller university, my general education requirements would be fulfilled in classrooms with a small group of my peers taught by a professor, rather than in a lecture hall filled with hundreds of students and a graduate assistant. While there is nothing at all wrong with big or small classes, it is something one should consider when determining where to go to school and whether to take some general electives at the community college back home during the summer. In the end, it really just comes down to your personal preference and learning style.

Also keep in mind your professors. Many of my classmates use Web sites such as www.ratemyprofessors.com when choosing which professor to select for a certain course. This Web site allows current and former students to post their opinions concerning how the professor rates in terms of ease, clarity, helpfulness, and quality. By reviewing other people's opinions, you will have an idea as to whether you want a certain professor. A few words of caution to keep in mind when using this service: many times, people who struggle with a class and receive poor grades are the ones who put negative reviews on the Web site. In many cases, the negative comments outweigh the good because students don't think to praise good professors. Face it, it's easier to complain about the bad things in life, especially when it can be done anonymously in an online forum. Too often we forget to be thankful for all of the good things God gives us, including great professors. We need to keep in mind the words of 1 Thessalonians 5:11, "Encourage one another and build one another up."

Trying to coordinate your schedule with a friend's adds to the complexity of registration. Is it better to take classes with your friends or without them? In reality, there are a number of things to consider when deciding to include friends in selecting your course schedule. On the positive side, if you sign up to be in the same course session with your friends, you will not walk into your first day of class without knowing someone. If it's a friend you enjoy hanging out with, you gain the advantage of an instant study partner and someone to motivate you when things get tough. If you have to miss class, you automatically have a friend who can share notes with you and explain ideas to you.

Having a friend in the same class is not without its downfalls, however. Some friends want to take advantage of your friendship and copy your work. Sometimes, academic settings prove to be competitive arenas, so instead of competing against your peers, you end up competing against your friends. You two may also seem like a clique to the rest of your classmates, and that could prevent you from meeting new people.

What you need to keep in mind is that you are attending a college or university to work toward your future, not theirs. Your schedule decision should be based on what is best for you, not what works best for them. When I moved away from home to college, I didn't know a single person at school. It was through the classroom that I met the people who are now my best friends. We do take some classes together, but for others, we go our separate ways. I always try to keep in mind the words of Colossians 3:23, "Whatever you do, work heartily, as for the Lord and not for men." I know that my purpose on earth is to serve the Lord, thanking Him for the talents and gifts He has given me. Though having classes with my friends is fun, I know that what I'm doing should be pleasing to God and benefiting my journey toward serving Him, not benefiting what my friends want.

I've not met one person who has absolutely loved his or her schedule. There is always something that won't seem as perfect as you'd like, but you can make the most of the experience and focus on the positive things that come with it. Registration day is over. You met your adviser and developed your class schedule. If something ends up not working out, there is always room for change. When you're registering, ask about the school's change policy. Most schools are out to impress first-year students because they want them to be successful and return the next year. Many schools will go out of their way to make sure first-year students are happy. So remember to weigh your options and do what works best for you!

Changing Your Major

If you are second-guessing or still have no idea what to do with your life, there are plenty of resources to help you. Many of my friends who have changed majors found that speaking to their advisers was beneficial. Though most schools assign faculty advisers based on your major, don't be afraid to speak to your assigned adviser regarding your concerns. Even though you think she might get upset that you're not choosing "her" major anymore, nothing could be further from the truth. Your adviser is a resource for you—advisers want you to be successful in school and your future career.

Many schools also offer career counselors to help you weigh your options. These counselors are trained to work with students who are looking for a career path but aren't sure where that path might lead. Several of my friends have taken something called the STRONG Interest Inventory when they went to see the career counselor. This inventory showed them things about themselves that they already knew but hadn't quite yet pieced together. Even though I was somewhat skeptical of the test's effectiveness, when I started doubting my choice of occupational therapy, I took the test too. The test results placed the two ideas I had for my future career side by side. Before taking the test, I was split between professional mission work and occupational therapy, but I never considered combining the two. When I got my results, I realized that maybe the answer all along was not that I had to pick between them, but rather, put them together. My time spent with the career counselor was probably the best time I spent throughout my struggle of "what should I do." My counselor knew a little about every job available out there. I've never had a friend complain once that counselors will not strive to find out what they don't know.

Friends and family also provide good insights, but I hesitate to say that sometimes they are not the best source of advice for what you should do when you grow up. Sometimes family members want to share what they think will be best for you. Family members sometimes forget that what is best for you is ultimately your decision.

Figuring out the answer may take some time and effort, but it will all play out. God has His plan for you; Psalm 139:16 says, "Your eyes saw my unformed substance; in Your book were written, every one of them, the days that were formed for me, when as yet there was none of them." So whether or not you know what you want to do now or as you enter college, it's all right! Keep working toward your goal, even if you're not completely sure about the direction.

Christ in the Classroom

You're in college now, and what happens in the classroom isn't as tightly controlled as it was in high school. By this I don't mean that there are more spit wads and chaos flying around; I mean that the viewpoints expressed by your college instructor are bound less by the government and more so by the university guidelines. Sure, in your public high school, evolution was a required teaching, but teachers generally were careful not to express their personal opinions. College is a whole new world when it comes to personal expression. Teachers may teach what they need to teach for the course requirements, but all of a sudden, their personal twists and perspectives come into play. It's intimidating because in your mind, you have to wonder, If I argue with this teacher, will my grade be affected? What will others think?

There is a story told of a professor from a state university teaching a class in which the sole objective was to prove that there was no God. A few students chose to take this class, while others were required to take it. In this class, the professor spent the semester proving to the students that there couldn't possibly be a God. On the last day of class, he instructed the class of three hundred students to stand up if there was anyone who still believed in God. For the twenty years he had taught this class, no one had ever stood up. To drive his point home, the professor proceeded to throw a piece of chalk on the ground saying that if there was a God, then He could keep the piece of chalk from shattering when it dropped to the ground, but it never happened.

In the twenty-first year of the class, a student came into the class only because it was required. He prayed every morning before class for the strength to defend his faith if needed. Sure enough, the last day of class came, and when the professor asked his famous question, that one student stood up alone and silent. The professor screamed, "You fool, if there was a God then He could save this piece of chalk from shattering into hundreds of pieces when I throw it to the ground." As the professor went to throw the chalk in his usual fashion, it slipped from his hands and rolled down his pant leg, onto his shoe, and then to the ground safe and sound. He silently walked out of the classroom. The student who stood up proceeded to tell his classmates about the grace and love of Jesus Christ.

In Matthew 16:24, Jesus asks us to deny ourselves and follow Him no matter the circumstance. At the same time, He promises that He will always be with us. We are called to be faithful in Christ, but we should also never forget He is always faithful to us. You may never find yourself in this type of situation, but if you are, take joy in the opportunity you have to share Christ. "But in your hearts honor Christ the Lord as holy, always being prepared to make a defense to anyone who asks you for a reason for the hope that is in you; yet do it with gentleness and respect" (1 Peter 3:15). There's so much more to say about this topic that this book has a whole chapter on what it means to live as a Christian on a secular campus. Check it out!

More on the Classroom Experience

The college classroom experience tends to be different from what you experienced in high school. I hate to say it, but in college you'll likely find professors who don't care much about you personally. They may not know your name or care whether you are passing the course. The course content will be more difficult, and you may need to make some adjustments to get into the proper routine. Procrastination needs to come out of your vocabulary in order to be successful, and studying habits will probably need to be a bit different than what you are used to. Your professors may have high expectations for what you can accomplish, sometimes within a small time frame. In order to be successful, you are expected to push beyond what you thought was your capacity. Though this seems overwhelming at first, it is a big part of adjusting to the college experience. Soon enough, you will be a professional at it!

It takes a lot of patience to deal with professors who are difficult to get along with or who don't care about their students. When you're sitting in a lecture hall with several hundred other students, the grad assistants don't have the time to get to know you. If you missed class, they probably wouldn't realize it. If your grades are starting to fall, the profs might assume that you aren't cut out for college. You have to be ready for these kinds of reactions. Whatever the task involving your courses, strive to do your very best and make use of God's gifts to you.

Don't get me wrong—there are professors out there who care. But it is more difficult to establish relationships with professors because of large class sizes. In most cases, professors post office hours during which you can meet and/or visit with the professors, discuss grades and expectations. In reality, many care, but with large class sizes, at times it's hard to tell.

In smaller universities, dealing with professors tends to be different. They often know you by name, realize when your grades are slipping, and notice when you're not in class. Part of being prepared for the learning experience includes completing assigned readings for each class period and reviewing discussions. A well-trained professor will recognize your level of preparation and grade your participation accordingly.

Peter reminds us that in that we should "always [be] prepared to make a defense to anyone who asks you for a reason for the hope that is in you; yet do it with gentleness and respect, having a good conscience, so that, when you are slandered, those who revile your good behavior in Christ may be put to shame" (1 Peter 3:15–16). The classroom should be a reflection of our lives as Christians. In the world, we must be prepared to defend our faith in Christ; in the classroom, we must be prepared to defend a topic at hand and be knowledgeable about it. As Christians, you need to speak with positive attitude and spirit, while at the same time remembering that you're in college for a reason. You are there to learn and grow; you should never be afraid to attack ideas, but be careful not to attack people.

Academic expectations vary widely from class to class. Some professors give you only a midterm and a final; other professors quiz you every class period; still others expect numerous writing assignments. Many professors, on the first day of class, provide you with a syllabus outlining all of the assignments for the semester. Others are like the professor my friend had who assigned the biggest project of the semester just two weeks before it was due. I watched her labor over that project day-after-day, sleepless night after sleepless night. Professors' deadlines are generally hard and fast. You may be able to get an extension on a larger project, but don't count on it. Professors assume that you are old enough to manage your time and workload responsibly.

Group projects are frequently an expectation in college classes. For me personally, group assignments are one of the most dreaded parts of college, yet at the same time, one of the best. I'm such a perfectionist that it is hard for me to allow others to take part in an assignment in fear that it won't get done to my standards. I often need to remind myself of the words of Ephesians 4:1–2, "Walk in a manner worthy of the calling to which you have been called, with all humility and gentleness, with patience, bearing with one another in love." For group work to be successful, you have to learn to share roles and form a team. Sit down and discuss personal strengths and weaknesses with one another and then outline a list of tasks that will be best for each group member. You will still be working together, but will be doing what best fits your gifts. Group assignments provide a great opportunity to develop teamwork skills and learn from other people, even though at times it can prove to be a challenge.

When working on group projects, make sure the members contribute equally, especially if you get a team member who seems to lack motivation and guidance. Never allow a group member to get away with not contributing. In my first group project in college, one girl never came to class or contributed to discussions or did any part of the group work. Then she tried to place her name on the finished product. I went immediately to my professor to talk about the situation; the girl was asked to do the project completely on her own or get a zero for the assignment.

Most professors and schools do not take cheating lightly. Always stand up for the work that you do, and never let anyone take advantage of it. In Ephesians 4:28, Paul writes, "Let the thief no longer steal, but rather let him labor, doing honest work with his own hands, so that he may have something to share with anyone in need." By giving someone credit for work that he or she doesn't do, you are in reality cheating yourself and society. The purpose of college is to gain knowledge so that you might serve a successful role in the world and with that role, serve God. If someone manages to cheat his way through college, he won't have something to share with those in need.

The college classroom can be any variety of things. You may have a prof who is fantastic or completely unprofessional. You might hang on every word your prof says or feel like you're taking away nothing from the experience. You could feel that a class is too hard or that the teacher is unreasonable or dry. Whatever you come across during your journey through college, remember to keep your head up. Pray to God about your experiences—ask for guidance or just thank Him when things are going well. Remember also, it is only a semester. There are always more classes and professors ahead of you. Do your best—that is all you have to give.

Seeking Help

You're in college. You're supposed to do well in all of your classes and you shouldn't need help along the way. For some of you, this may be true, but not for all. Not everyone is gifted at everything. You're in college to learn more, and sometimes, your classes may prove difficult. You may struggle with them, not do as well as you'd like, and possibly even fail a class or two, but this does not have to be the case—if you're willing to work a little more.

Most colleges have some form of tutoring services available, and many provide this service at no cost to the student. "Tutor?" "What?" "I don't need a tutor!" "It's embarrassing to go to a tutor!" "I'm not that dumb!" I bet these thoughts are running through your head right now; at one time, they ran through mine. Going to a tutor doesn't make you dumb. If anything, going to a tutor actually makes you smarter than those who choose not to go to a tutor at all. By getting help through a tutor, you are making one of the smartest choices of your college career. If you're making an A already, still go! There is always more to learn and helpful tips to get more out of course material. If you're making a B, go! You may be able to pull that up to an A. If you're failing, then definitely go! You don't want to start your college career by being put on academic probation and risk being kicked out of school or a specialty program, so seek help to work through your difficulties.

I work as tutor for my school. Not only do I tutor other students but I also receive tutoring myself. In fact, there are quite a few tutors in the Academic Success Center who receive tutoring. It's common to be strong at one subject but not in another. Tutors not only help you learn and understand course material better but they also give you tips to form better study habits and skills. James 1:5 says, "If any of you lacks wisdom, let him ask God, who gives generously to all without reproach, and it will be given him." God does indeed grant us wisdom, but we are still fallen humans. Some of the wisdom from God is that which has us seeking help in our struggles. Don't be afraid to get a tutor. It doesn't mean you are dumb or anything of the sort. It means you are wise enough to ask for help. With a little work, you could see an improvement in much of what you are learning and understanding, and your grades should reflect it. God will be with you through your journey, but He won't just hand you the answers. He expects us to study diligently and seek help when needed, for this is true wisdom.

Using Technology as a Learning Device

The world is changing, and college students are some of the most technologically literate individuals. Because of the surge of technology into our lives, the computer is an active part of learning on all levels. Many institutes of higher education push professors to incorporate technology into the everyday routine of the classroom. Assignments are turned in online, some quizzes and tests are taken online, and student-to-instructor communication is commonly via e-mail. For some students, it can be a big adjustment initially, but the electronic habit forms quickly, and then it seems strange to turn in a hard copy.

Many classes use a Web Course Tool program (WebCT) such as Blackboard or Desire2Learn. Even if the class is not designated as an online class, many professors use the programs to post grades, the syllabus, assignments, and other course content. They may also put up out-of-class discussions or even have you take a test online so that you get instant feedback. Online discussions can be great tools for students who are too shy to feel comfortable with normal classroom discussions and confrontations. On the computer, they have time to think through ideas and react to other people's opinions. Since you are sharing your opinions, however, remember that everyone can see them and to keep them appropriate and Christ pleasing. Sadly, many people do not watch what they say in online discussions and use the slang and jargon that they use in everyday life—which tends to be inappropriate in most class settings. Some may also find it tempting to work on online coursework with friends who are in the same class. Sure, it sounds like a good idea, but you will likely get caught and may be punished.

If your class never meets in a classroom and is strictly an online class, you have to manage your time well; otherwise, you can fall behind very quickly. It's easy to put off projects when there isn't a constant reminder (like a classroom and professor that you meet with regularly) of fast-approaching deadlines. You may also think that you will be able to find all of the answers in the book for online classes. Although this may seem like a good idea, if you've not prepared ahead of time, you will be too busy searching for answers and will run out of time to complete the test. Online classes still require time for studying! It made me cringe to watch my roommate on the computer cramming during the final minutes before a fifteen-minute quiz was due. There was no room for errors on her part, no time for mistakes—just a clock clicking down because of her failure to prioritize. Make the best use of your time. It is the key to success!

E-mail Communication

Professionalism, professionalism, professionalism! That is the key to online communication with everyone, especially professors! I listened to a professor speak once about her course syllabus. In the syllabus, she specifically wrote that if e-mails were directed to her and were not professional or complete, grammatically correct sentences, she would send back a reply stating the student should see "page five, paragraph four of the syllabus," which explains the need for a more formal, proper e-mail. For example:

BAD E-MAIL:
hey dr. cap, i wasnt sure about wat u were wanting turned in next class. is it ok if ya just explain it again in class Monday? Thanx a million, jane

GOOD E-MAIL:
Dr. Capstone, I am unclear about the assignment that you gave us today in class that is due on Monday. Can I please schedule a time to meet with you to discuss your expectations? I noticed your office hours run on Thursday from noon to four. Will one-thirty work? Otherwise, just let me know the best time to meet

with you, and I will work around your schedule. Regards, Jane Doe, MWF General Psychology 101, 10:50 A.M.

Notice the difference between a professionally written communication versus how you would IM your best friend. It is good to get into the practice of communicating professionally now with your professors, because when you are an employee, it will be expected of you.

Another thing to keep in mind is that e-mail will probably be the primary means of communication between your professors, you, and the university. Make a habit of checking your e-mail at least once daily. Some professors like to add assignments at the last minute; these are still due because "you should've been responsible and checked your e-mail."

Keeping Your Online Life Professional

MySpace, Facebook, and Twitter. These are some of the most common social networking sites available to students. They are free and provide great ways to stay in touch with friends and people who care about you, but you need to be cautious about what you post. Future employers have access to your profile. It saddens me to see many of my classmates' Facebook profiles with pictures of a sexual nature or showing drinking, and partying. Employers look down on those habits, as does our heavenly Father. Remember that the best way to have a profile is to do so in a Christian manner.

 a.w.

nine

Where Has All the Time Gone?

Where has all the time gone!? It's a phrase that we hear over and over again. You wake up, try to fit as much in as possible, and then go back to sleep. The average person should sleep about eight hours a day, so that leaves you with two-thirds of what we call a day left, and it seems to fly by! It would be great if we were able to view time as God does; to Him, "one day is as a thousand years, and a thousand years as one day" (2 Peter 3:8). But this is far from the case for us, especially when it comes to college. It's important to set up routines, priorities, and schedules to allocate how best to use your time and how to handle all of the tasks presented to you. College isn't about all work and no fun, but it is likewise not about all play and no work. Being a college student is a full-time job in which you are investing money. Learning time management is one of the keys in achieving success.

IIIIIIIIIIIIIIIIIIIIIIIIIIIII

Setting Priorities

One of the most important things to learn when you begin college is that you have to set priorities. You set yourself up for failure if you do not begin to do this early in the game. It will take a good deal of time and effort to keep ahead of the game, but it doesn't take much to get behind. Before school even starts, you should consider all of the elements that weigh in on your time, such as class, homework, social activities, work, sports, and time with God. Make a list of these things and try to calculate how much of your time you plan to devote to each activity. Try to avoid the temptation to make time with God a low priority. Jesus reminds us, "Seek first the kingdom of God and His righteousness" (Matthew 6:33). By putting God first, the rest of our priorities fall into place.

As college students, our academics need to follow closely. Believe it or not, college is not as much about the social experience as some people think. It is about preparing yourself to be successful in your future career. I have many friends who make a schedule of classes and locations and post it to their door. Not only does it help them stay on track, but whenever I see their packed schedule, I understand the need to give them space. If the schedule says they are free, then I know it's okay to stop in and visit.

You may think that college is going to be just like high school and that you will have plenty of time to do whatever you want. College is not like that at all. You will no longer be attending class from eight until three Monday through Friday. Your class times will be scattered throughout the week; you will have more homework. You will have work and meetings to attend, and you will need to be self-motivated to complete the tasks. No class until one in the afternoon? Great! This does not mean sleeping until noon; it means keeping a balanced schedule and accomplishing things early on in the day to clear room later in your day for other events and activities. The morning is a perfect time for doing homework, reading, or even surfing the Internet. The earlier you develop strong study habits and optimize the use of your time, the better off you will be.

When you don't prioritize, there could be some hefty consequences. If you make poor use of your time, in all likelihood you are staying up too late trying to make up for procrastinating. Your lack of sleep leads to a shorter attention span, poor grades, and poorer health. You end up disappointing other people such as your parents, your teachers who saw your potential, and yourself when you realize the depth of the hole you have dug for yourself. Priorities, priorities, priorities. These are the keys to healthy time management.

Academics

One of the most important roles in time management encompasses academia. You will have *so* much else to do, but you must remember not to push your schoolwork aside. A full-time course load runs between twelve and eighteen credit hours of classroom time per week, but this does not include time spent studying. Most experts recommend anywhere from two to four hours of study per credit hour outside of the classroom to keep up with the course requirements. If we use the middle range of the scale, a person with fifteen credit hours ends up spending forty-five hours minimum per week on coursework, plus the fifteen hours spent in the classroom. If you sleep eight hours per night, that takes fifty-six more of your hours per week. This leaves you fifty-two hours in a week to do everything else. The basic activities of daily living take up a large chunk of these hours. If you spend too much time doing other things, you may notice a decline in the amount of time you should be dedicating to your studies.

One of the things I clearly remember during new student orientation was the director of the Academic Success Center telling us that we would procrastinate something very bad only one time before we never did it again. I laughed at this idea, and then began my freshman year by procrastinating on almost every single assignment that came my way. While I heard these instructions, I did not listen to them. Procrastinating worked for a while, but then I put off a very large assignment until the day before it was due. I expected the library to have everything I needed for the project. When I searched the school's online library, it appeared as if all of the resources were available. This, however, was not the case. The day before I needed to turn in my assignment, there I was, without any peer-reviewed articles to write my paper, and I needed six. I slept a little over one hour that night. I worked very hard and ultimately did come up with enough that would do for the assignment, but "just making do" is all it did. The director was right. All it should take is one close call or bad mistake, and you will realize that procrastination is not the key to doing well in college.

Had I not finished the assignment, I would still have ended up in class the next morning to face the consequences. With some professors, the consequences would result in a zero on the assignment. A slightly better-case scenario would mean a reduction in my grade. The old saying goes "you get what you deserve." As college students, you are expected to be responsible for yourself and your own actions (or lack of action).

I was often frustrated to see how one of my roommates managed to get "sick" on days major assignments were due. I was even more frustrated to hear how frequently her instructors fell for her excuses and allowed extensions. She got lucky. Most instructors are not so lenient.

When preparing an assignment for class, allow yourself ample time to finish the work. If you start early and allow yourself plenty of time, you will be prepared and still be able to finish the assignment if something unexpected happens. Proverbs 27:1 reminds us, "Do not boast about tomorrow, for you do not know what a day may bring." You may make plans to do an assignment the day before it is due, but what happens when you get into an accident, get sick, or something else comes up? Preparedness is the key.

Another bad habit I see is classmates skipping class for some reason or another—most frequently due to a lack of sleep the night before. I once calculated how much money would be lost if I were to skip just one class period. Granted, I attend a private university with higher than average tuition, but this calculation serves as a good indicator of the loss that comes with not attending. If you take fifteen credit hours, this typically means five classes in a semester. Each class normally meets two times per week for an hour and fifteen minutes. That equals ten class sessions per week for the sixteen weeks of the semester, making roughly 160 class periods per semester. With that figure and approximately $10,000 tuition per semester, that's just over $60 per class session. Is it really worth losing that much money just to miss one class? The cost of skipping class builds up quickly—financially, academically, and otherwise.

IIIIIIIIIIIIIIIIIIIIIIIIIII

Your Job

The time required for course work alone in college compares to having a full-time job. Even though students face increasing expenses and a tightening financial system, holding a job may not be the best idea to counteract the problem. Using the calculations mentioned earlier, a person has fifty-two hours left over each week. Some of this time may be allocated for a job. For some people, working is the only way to pay for college. If you need to work while attending college, consider carefully how you use your time. It is possible to work, but you must be conscious of time; otherwise, your schoolwork could quickly become neglected.

There are several types of jobs college students typically hold: jobs back home, off-campus jobs, on-campus jobs, and work-study jobs; some types of jobs might even be combined. Each comes with its own benefits and pitfalls. Whatever your case may be, remember to watch your time and how you schedule yourself, especially during your first semester of college. If at all possible, allow yourself an adjustment period to see how you handle the academic schedule before adding work hours on top of it. If you handle your course load okay, then picking up some hours at work is probably an okay thing to do.

One of the most common jobs a student will have is a work-study job, which is based on financial need and funded through the government. On average students work five to ten hours per week, and the money can either be applied toward tuition or a paycheck. Work-study jobs are usually quite flexible. Many people who have an hour or two break between classes fill that time slot working. This all depends on the supervisor and department in which you are placed, but supervisors typically allow students to fill in hours because they understand their busy class schedule. It is possible to work on campus without being awarded work-study funds, but it is less common. To find these opportunities, inquire with the human resource department at your school or watch for flyers advertising special opportunities or help wanted.

Unless you are fortunate, you will lose a lot of flexibility with working a job off campus. When applying for a job, clearly specify what kind of time you can commit to or need. Whatever jobs you hold now will eventually be on a résumé, so make sure you keep on a positive note with your supervisor because someday you may need him or her as a reference. Off-campus jobs typically add a commute, so make sure you plan accordingly. If you plan your time well, you should have time to work at least a few hours a week. A lot of places are in great need of weekend workers, so having a weekend job is always a possibility, and it will probably mesh better with your school schedule as well.

For me, I have never held a job off campus except when I was home—about two hours away from campus. I have been with the same employer while away at school by serving on an "as needed" basis. They schedule me when I am home for breaks. This allows me to make some extra cash during extended semester breaks and also guarantees that I will have a summer job. Though this scenario may not work for everybody, it is something worth checking into as a possibility. As long as you work hard and they have a need for workers, most employers will likely be willing to keep you on staff. Having a job like this allows you to concentrate on your course work at school and work when school is not in session. The biggest caution with this type of job arrangement is that you miss out on time with your family when you are home.

||||||||||||||||||||||||||

Campus Life

What's college without having some fun? The answer: it's not. You could go through college by attending classes and staying in the library the rest of the day, but that's not necessarily a good plan either. Having a good time, within moderation, and being involved is something that every college student should do. But having fun shouldn't distract from your focus on studies or from God. Your activities should reflect positive, Christian values. While being involved in activities is a good thing, make sure the activities are appropriate. Spending all your free time drinking at parties is probably the worst way to use your time. The Bible clearly speaks against drunkenness and other similar acts. These acts have a negative impact not only on your time but also on your life. There are plenty of other things to get involved with on campus that are not against the written moral code presented in the Bible. Between clubs, dorm life, and sports, a person is pretty much set with positive things to do!

Within your campus community, you are likely to find a club of every kind! Schools offer a large variety of clubs, and they often encourage you to create your own if one you would like to see doesn't already exist. It is good to become actively involved in at least one organization while on campus because it is a good way to make connections with other students and a good way to show your support for something that interests you. I know several people who have become very active in so many student organizations that their time is completely engulfed due to over-involvement. They are so busy running from event to event that they miss out on participating in the events because they are too busy planning them. I'll admit that I've at times taken on too much involvement; consequently, I've had to think about which activities mean the most to me, which ones I like to help plan, and which ones I would be happy just attending. By weighing these options, I am able to be active in the things I am passionate about and still enjoy the other events on campus. You don't have to be in an organization to attend an event sponsored by it. By simply attending, you can enjoy yourself on your own time. You have to learn moderation and be reasonable about what kind of time commitment you have to offer.

On top of student organizations, you have activities happening right on your dormitory floor. This was perhaps my greatest weakness when it came to time management during my freshman year of college. It was so easy to head to the lounge on my floor to have a "study group" that actually turned into movie marathons and social hours. Though dorm life is important and fun, it is also something you have to be careful with because there is so much going on that it is easy to get distracted from the things you should be doing. At the same time, you shouldn't coop yourself inside of your room all of the time either. It is good to socialize with your roommates and your friends next door; you just have to remember to watch your time and priorities carefully. If my friends are in their rooms studying or just lounging around, they normally leave the door open to be inviting. This made the dorms a more homelike environment, and it gave the students time to get things done but still be sociable.

Perhaps the busiest activities on campus revolve around sports. Whether you are the fan or the dedicated or recreational athlete, being involved with sports can be a rewarding way to spend your time. As with all things, athletics must be carefully planned into your schedule. There will be a lot of time dedicated to practice, games, travel, and even to extra rest. When adding this to your academic load, your time is pretty much fully committed. To be involved in athletics, a certain grade-point average is typically required, so using your times and breaks wisely are necessary. If you play sports for recreation, such as with intramural sports, then you will still have time committed to practicing and a night or two of games per week, but it is much less intense than the typical athlete who will be practicing and playing almost every day of the week. The benefit of being a fan is that you don't have to attend the game unless you choose to do so. It is, however, a good social event to attend and is a great way to show off some school spirit!

Spirituality and Campus Ministry

"Let us run with endurance the race that is set before us, looking to Jesus, the founder and perfecter of our faith" (Hebrews 12:1–2). In our everyday lives, we have opportunities to spend time with our Lord and Savior as we seek His guidance and learn to live by His Word. However, with the busy schedules most college students face, it is often easy to set Jesus aside. Sunday morning rolls around, and it may be the only chance you get all week to sleep in. God will understand this time, you say. But one time leads to another, and habits slowly begin to form. Suddenly, Sunday worship is missing from your life, and you begin to fall away from God. You may think that this won't happen to you. So did I, but I found myself wandering away from Christ during my first semester of college. Sadly, this is the case with many students who go away to college. They never make a spiritual connection, so they end up losing one altogether. It took a lot to make me see that maybe life was not going so great because something great was missing from it. Romans 10:17 reminds us, "Faith comes from hearing, and hearing through the word of Christ." Without hearing and learning God's Word, you can become lost. Making time for worship with fellow Christians is something I urge you to make a priority.

A big thing for me was that I never had anyone to go to church with, and I lacked the motivation to go on my own. Though there was no excuse for me to quit going, it happened, and sometimes I feel that had I made a connection with someone to go to church with earlier on, perhaps I would not have lost my focus. When I realized what I was missing in my life, I found a local congregation. I asked a friend to join me on the first weekend I went, even though she was of a different denomination. My friend and I lived three doors apart all year, and neither of us attended church because we didn't have anyone to go with. Now we both attend the same church every Sunday and have really enjoyed growing in our faith through Christ, growing together as friends, and growing in our connection with the congregation. We began scheduling events around our time with God rather than scheduling time with God around our events.

There is, however, a lot more to keeping God in focus in your schedule. This is something you need to keep in mind. Find times in your schedule to read your Bible, pray, and reflect on the blessings God has given you. I'll admit that this never struck me as too important until one day when I was talking to a friend who had spent a lot of time on mission trips, and he told me that when he was on his trips, he learned to begin every day with God. In doing so, he found that his days ran much smoother and he was in a better mood. Better days? Of course, I'm going to do whatever it takes to have a better day right off the bat! He was right. I try to start my days with God every day, and it truly does make things go better. It gives me strength in times of weakness and encouragement to continue to live my life according to God's will. During the day, I reflect on what I have read and find ways to apply it to my life. Keeping God in your schedule is the most important thing to do. Without God, what is the meaning behind everything else?

Putting focus on campus ministry within your schedule is perhaps one of the greatest ways to keep Christ with you on campus. By leaving room in your schedule for campus ministry involvement, you will connect with people of similar beliefs and be able to worship and socialize with them. It will be encouraging for you to see your time spent with people who believe what you do; it will be encouraging to know that you are not alone no matter how big or little the campus might be. "We know that for those who love God all things work together for good, for those who are called according to His purpose" (Romans 8:28).

||||||||||||||||||||||||||

Friends and Family Back Home

It almost seems as though there won't be time for family and friends once school begins, especially if you are leaving them back home. This is not the case. Will you be able to call home every single day? Probably not, and you really shouldn't. College is about learning, and one of those learning experiences is to gain independence and responsibilities. It is good to stay connected back home, but at the same time, remember to think through challenges on your own and remember that some stories are worth saving. Your parents understand when you don't call them every day, but do try to include them more often than once every few months. They like to know what's going on in your life, but this needs to be done in moderation. Your parents love you and want what is best for you. They want to boast about your accomplishments—they are proud of you. They want to hear that you are spending your time wisely and to God's glory, and they want reassurance that all of the money they are helping you out with isn't going to waste. You should respect those wishes; they have raised you with the hopes that you do your very best. By managing your time and schedules wisely, you will be on the road to giving your parents great joy.

Most likely, you've left many of your friends back home as well, or they have headed off to different schools. Whatever the case, you don't have to lose them as friends. You have a lot less time together, so it's important to schedule times for you to reconnect, especially when you are home. Invite friends to come to events on campus that you think might interest them. My sister was on a school trip during Siblings Weekend, but I wanted someone from home to join me. Even though the weekend is oriented toward younger siblings, I invited my best friend from home to come join me—we had an amazing time. It gave us a chance to be together in the environment in which I had grown accustomed. If you plan carefully, things in your schedule can overlap in a positive way. I am fortunate that my campus is fairly close to home. That may not be the case with you, however, but there are other ways to stay in touch with your friends from home, and most of them are due to one of our favorite friends—technology.

Staying in touch with family and friends is easier than ever before. They are just a text, phone call, e-mail, or Facebook post away. You can share your life moments with everyone at once instead of individually, thus saving precious time. Yet they need to understand that you will be busy and may not be available some days because of your schedule. When you have free time, let them know that they are important to you and that you want to include them in your life as much as possible.

||||||||||||||||||||||||||||

A Time for Everything

Ecclesiastes 3:1–8 is probably the greatest summary of time management:

> *For* everything there is a season, and a time for every matter under heaven: a time to be born, and a time to die; a time to plant, and a time to pluck up what is planted; a time to kill, and a time to heal; a time to break down, and a time to build up; a time to weep, and a time to laugh; a time to mourn, and a time to dance; a time to cast away stones, and a time to gather stones together; a time to embrace, and a time to refrain from embracing; a time to seek, and a time to lose; a time to keep, and a time to cast away; a time to tear, and a time to sew; a time to keep silence, and a time to speak; a time to love, and a time to hate; a time for war, and a time for peace.

There is a time for everything within our lives, especially in college. There is going to be a time for studying and a time for relaxing. There are going to be times for fun but other times for work. There will be times when you can pick up extra responsibilities, and there will be other times when you are too committed to other things that you have to say no. You will need to set priorities and stick to them and be prepared for the consequences if you do not. There will be an adjustment period. Things are changing at a fast pace in your life, but God is with you, so remember Him in your daily journey, in the good times and in the struggles.

 a.w.

Christian on a Secular Campus

Let's take an imaginative leap here and pretend we're going camping with one hundred other young adults. (Some of you may have just checked out of this little make-believe world. *Stinging insects and days marinating in dirty sweat,* you say? *No thanks.* But read on anyway.) For our trip, each of us will be given a hand-drawn map, a knapsack, water bottle, packets of freeze-dried food, a box of bandages, and a mini roll of toilet paper (use sparingly or pray the leaves out there are larger than average). Our goal is to navigate miles of wilderness full of steep ravines, prowling bears, and irritable, trigger-happy mountain men who like to point travelers in the wrong direction. Oh, and only thirty-six of us will make it back.

That last sentence would do it in for most of us—a 64 percent chance of an untimely demise is not exactly a favorable prognosis, even for imaginary excursions. *You can keep your mini roll of toilet paper,* we'd say. *We'll just chill on the beach this time.* But even though it would be easy for you to duck out of a make-believe trip, almost everyone reading this will soon be heading off on a journey with very similar statistics for survival: 64 percent is a recent estimation of the number of young adults who lose touch with or turn their backs on their faith in college.

||||||||||||||||||||||||||||

First, a Few Clarifiers

It's important to note that no survey or study could ever measure the growth or loss of actual faith. Only God searches the heart, and only God knows the depth of a person's belief and love for Him. Someone who outwardly shows no signs of having a heart for Jesus might be praying to Him every night. Someone who appears to have forgotten all about salvation might simply be questioning what he or she believes and waiting to ask the right questions. What *can* be measured, however, is church attendance and religious involvement (youth group, choir, etc.). Current studies show that association with these activities plummets after high school, indicating a large number of Christians who are letting their relationship with God wither.

Another important fact about this mass faith degeneration is that college itself is not, I repeat, *not* the bad guy. Young adults who never enroll in college have similar, and in some cases even higher, levels of decline in church attendance. Researchers Mark D. Regnerus and Jeremy E. Uecker, both of the University of Texas, point out that, while it is true that religious involvement wanes for students attending universities, there is little support for the assumption that colleges *cause* this decline. Instead, involvement drops probably occur not because the university is a bad place (as some people falsely believe) but because *life changes drastically* for those graduating high school, whether they are planning

on attending college or not, and those changes, often unfore-
seen, result in people putting their faith in something other
than God.

Life Changes—
Getting a Grip on the Landscape

Let's talk a little about the specific dangers you might
face when you get to college—dangers that will pull you away
from being involved in faith-building activities. *Hey, wait a
minute,* you say, *you just told me college wasn't the bad guy!*
You're right, I did. But while college is not in itself the reason for turning from faith, it is the setting, the *landscape,* if
you will, for your journey through the changes coming your
way, and it presents some very unique challenges for a young
Christian. Also, if this really were a camping trip like we discussed earlier, you'd want to find out everything you could
about the geographic area you were heading into in order
to make sure you would be one of the thirty-six who made
it back. Here are some of the distractions and problems that
might try to ensure you *don't.*

It's a Self-Guided Tour—Sudden Responsibility

A lot of students don't realize the giant role their parents
played in their lives until they get to college and no longer
hear Dad's voice lecturing them about saving money and
Mom ordering them to change their socks every once in a
while, for Pete's sake. At college, you will have sole responsibility for making yourself get up to go to service on a Sunday
morning (or, alternatively, Saturday or Sunday *evening* services) or getting your homework out of the way so you can
attend that midweek Bible study (Chapter 9: Where Has All
the Time Gone? addresses some of these issues.) Jessa, a

student at Kansas State University, found out how difficult it was to leave her dorm room for church sometimes. "It was so easy to think I could just read my Bible a little longer and not go out," she says, "especially during the winter when it was really cold!" As a semi-independent adult, for the first time in your life you may also have to search for and decide which church you will attend, and that can be as daunting as being dropped in the middle of a forest with no compass.

Steep Ravines and Rushing Rivers—Temptations

You've already read in chapters 4 and 5 about many of the temptations that you might face—sex, alcohol, partying, and cheating on work are some of the most difficult things to avoid in college. It seems as though everyone is doing them and, like climbing down into a valley, you might not notice how low you've let yourself get until you look back up toward the top. Unfortunately, sometimes the climb back up looks so difficult (we're ashamed or guilty or afraid of how much we might have to change) that we decide to stay where we are, forgetting that if we reach out, someone we've been traveling with will throw us a lifeline and it will be worth all the effort in the end.

Lions and Tigers and . . . Okay, Okay, Sorry!—Scornful Friends

The heading is corny but the danger is real. Friends have an enormous impact on our thoughts, desires, and actions, and their influence and advice can be as comforting as a songbird or as poisonous as a rattlesnake. At college, you are guaranteed to meet and make friends with people who have very different backgrounds and beliefs than you, and sometimes they will strongly disagree with the Christian way of life. Friends may question the need for church attendance, chide you for making "holier than thou" moral choices, or even blatantly ridicule Christians, gnawing at your resolve and making it difficult to stick to what you know is right. When Elizabeth was at college at Fort Hays State University, she had some friends who would give her a hard time about going to church and praying instead of going out and having fun. "They would say that God shouldn't control my time, that He just watches what we do," she says. "I usually let them rant and then explained how much going to church meant to me, but it was hard to deal with at times."

Mountain Men (and Women)—Professors

We hear horror stories about professors who (like our rifle-wielding mountain men from the beginning) blast students with impossible questions, ridicule them in class, or hand out failing grades for good work, just because they find out the students are Christian. These professors truly exist and can be extremely intimidating; however, in most cases, you will find your professors to be at least polite if not kind, mostly fair, and extremely knowledgeable about their particular field. Unfortunately, these professors also present challenges, but in more subtle ways. A professor may calmly state a "scientific fact" that conflicts with the teaching of the Bible, or he or she may talk about religion as having social benefits similar to but no better than those of recycling. One professor of mine occasionally wore a T-shirt that read "Fairytale Creatures." It then listed about ten imaginary beings, beginning with Santa Clause and ending with—you guessed it—God. Because he was smart, likable, funny, and genuinely concerned about students' well-being, it was easy for my fellow students to comply with this professor's subtle direction *away* from the Creator of the universe and toward a wilderness they might never get out of.

City of Gold Dreams—Problems with Purpose

It seems like all the men who first explored America were looking for the same thing—gold. Preferably an entire *city* made of the stuff. (That was Coronado's dream, by the way. The guy was overflowing with optimism.) When they didn't find it, they were disappointed and struggled to make their reports back home sound positive. *No, we didn't find anything of value, really, but . . . ah . . . we staked out a nice hunk of land for a basket-weaving party and . . . um . . . discovered tomatoes. . . .* Little did those men know that the "hunk of land" they were so disappointed with would become one of the richest and most powerful countries in the world. They were so busy searching for one thing that they forgot to think about what might matter farther down the road.

This same phenomenon happens with college students today. They have been led to believe that building skills for a career, experiencing new things, making friends and connections, finding a spouse, or a combination of these, comprise the number one reason for attending college and therefore should occupy the greatest amount of their attention and energy. These goals are all healthy if properly sought after; however, they are *secondary goals*. Our *first* priority, in anything we do, is to serve God wholeheartedly. He doesn't want to be set aside while we jump-start our lives and then be picked up again once we have a family and cushy career. He wants to *be* our life *now*. Romans 9:17 says, "For this very purpose I have raised you up, that I might show My power in you, and that My name might be proclaimed in all the earth." Our purpose is to glorify Him. Now, this doesn't mean we should skip all our classes, shave our heads like monks, and meditate on Scripture twenty hours a day, but rather that we should stay connected to God so much that we make Him the biggest part of everything we do, right down to eating and drinking (1 Corinthians 10:31). Instead of searching for *gold* in this wilderness, we need to be searching for *God*.

||||||||||||||||||||||||||||

The Plan—Survival

Some of you had no idea that there were so many threatening factors of college life. Others of you may have heard about them over and over again or even faced them already in high school. But for all of you, the next logical question is this: *If that's what I'm up against, how do I make sure that I'll be able to get through it all?* Well, to stick with the camping trip analogy, what would you do to prepare for all the difficult challenges ahead if you were walking into the wilderness? Simple—you'd make a *plan*. You'd *prepare* for the difficulties ahead, because knowing about the dangers you might face does nothing for you unless you also know what you're going to do if and when you encounter them.

First off, you'd want to do some research, perhaps compiling a personal manual full of information and other useful knowledge about the terrain, wildlife, and so forth. Second, you'd stuff your knapsack with extra items that you might need (a full first-aid kit instead of just bandages, warm clothing and a poncho for rain, matches and a pot for boiling water, and most important, M&Ms and snickerdoodles). Finally, you might buy or rent a pair of heavy-duty walkie-talkies so you could pick up radio signals and call for help or advice.

‖‖‖‖‖‖‖‖‖‖‖‖‖‖‖‖‖‖‖‖‖‖‖‖

The Manual

Here are some ideas for some information and tools you might want to put in your own manual—resources and opportunities you should be aware of before you go to college so that you are ready to make use of them when the time comes.

Campus Christian Organizations

Getting involved with a Christian group on campus will give you an instant connection to other Christians your age and allow you to find some friends who are likely to help you strengthen your Christian faith rather than drag you away from it. Organizations will differ in size, style, and number, depending on where you go to school, but a typical campus group might feature weekly meetings with praise music and a message, fun weekend getaways, small-group Bible studies, and the chance to go on mission trips or help with community projects. A good way to discover which groups will be available to you is to get on your college Web site and look for a listing of religious organizations, then contact the leaders of several groups to ask what their mission statement is and what they try to accomplish.

Another way to select a group is to attend organization fairs on your campus or ask Christian upperclassmen which groups they prefer. When you have selected a few groups to try, *go* to them. Give each at least three weeks before you decide it is not for you—it will take a while before the uncomfortable feeling of being a newbie wears off. *Do note*, however, that sometimes an uncomfortable feeling arises because something is not right with the theology or practices of a group. If your instincts are sending you warning signals, recheck the mission statement, core beliefs, and leadership of the group to make sure "Christian" is a lifestyle and not just a label.

Church

While campus Christian groups and Bible studies are excellent faith-building opportunities and good ways to connect yourself with other students, they are *not* substitutes for regular church attendance. The instruction of an ordained pastor, the fellowship of Christians of all ages and experiences, and the administration of the Lord's Supper are all invaluable parts of a church service that it is difficult to find anywhere else. Still, a lot of college students find themselves attending church less and less often as the first year wears on, due to a variety of factors.

Sometimes the problem lies in simply finding a church, especially with students attending a university in a smaller town where there might be no churches in their denomination. If this happens to you, enlist your parents and/or pastor (use the walkie-talkie!). Ask them to help you find a church in your denomination. If none is available, ask for advice about which denominations have beliefs most similar to yours, and attend one or several of those churches with an open mind and the willingness to ask questions to understand your differences. Keep in mind that *any* church you attend will most likely be very different from your home church and you will have to get used to a new pastor, worship style, and congregation, but it will be worth the effort in the end.

Even after finding a church, some students still have difficulty making it to services. For example, some students have no way to get there. If you have no car or if using it is for some reason limited or difficult, call the pastor of the church you would like to attend and ask if there are families near where you live who would be willing to pick you up every Sunday. You can also check out the availability of public transportation in your town, or consider asking a friend with a car to drive you to church for a small fee or for dinner once a month (chances are, the person will not ask for much, if anything at all).

Finally, the biggest problem most college students face when struggling to attend church might be simply finding the motivation to get up and *go.* If you worry that you will not have the self-discipline to be consistent in your attendance, *commit* yourself to something. Join the praise team, bell choir, or band, sign up for ushering or greeting, volunteer to watch children in the nursery or teach Sunday School—anything that will cause someone to depend on you and therefore give you one more reason to go. Another helpful tactic is to ask one or several friends to go with you and hold you accountable for making it to church every Sunday. Even though Jason, a student at Hanover College in Indiana, found early services difficult to attend, he motivated himself by going to church with a group of people. "I knew they would be disappointed with me if I wasn't there," he said, "and that helped me get up in the morning."

Apologetics Resources

As you may know, apologetics has nothing to do with being sorry for wrecking your little brother's tricycle at the bottom of Dead Man's Hill or using your mom's cashmere sweater to put out the microwave fire. Instead, apologetics indicates "a formal justification or defense." In other words, any time you engage in discussion about your faith with a skeptical friend or professor, you are doing apologetics yourself. Defending Christianity can seem like a giant task, but there are ways to prepare for questions that come your way, namely:

- Know *what* you believe

- Know *why* you believe it

- Know what you *don't know*

- Know *how* to find out

If you've never done it before, try writing out your own creed or answering some simple questions on your own time, starting with something as basic as "Is there a God?" or "Is the Christian God the true God?" and getting more specific, like "What is the purpose for Baptism?" And always end your questions by asking *why* you hold that specific belief. (For example, I believe there is a God *because* of the complexity and beauty of the universe, because of the existence of truth and a need for a source for it, because I have studied the history and prophecy of the Bible and believe it to be the best answer for the evidence of God and all things, and because, after believing all this, I have seen God's presence in my life in countless ways.) Knowing what you believe and why will help you tremendously in situations where you might otherwise end up saying something like, "Um . . . well I guess I believe because my parents . . . ah . . . told me so . . . and they're really cool, mostly . . . except on family vacations or when I break curfew. . . ."

When you get to the point in your questions where you are no longer able to come up with strong, reasonable answers (say, for instance, you're not sure why you trust that the Gospels are the truth and not just wishful thinking), don't get down. Start asking! Make your life a quest to better know God and what you believe. Pick something you don't understand and ask pastors and knowledgeable adults, look for Web sites and books on the subject (for the truth of the Gospels and information about Jesus, look for Lee Strobel's book *A Case for Christ,* available in full and student editions), and most of all, search the Scriptures for insight. Use this same strategy when you meet with questions or even ridicule from friends and professors—if you don't know, simply tell them you're learning and you'll try to find out. Keep in mind that sometimes answers won't come easy; but check out Ephesians 3:20–21 for some encouragement:

> *Now* to Him who is able to do far more abundantly than all that we ask or think, according to the power at work within us, to Him be glory in the church and in Christ Jesus throughout all generations, forever and ever. Amen.

The Trip—Putting the Plan into Action

You can probably guess what this section will be about. Once you've researched the area you'll be traveling in, become aware of the problems you might face, and compiled tools and information to help you deal with those problems when they occur, there is nothing left to do but start walking. Your journey is about to begin.

It is logical to assume that, since you've read so far into this book, you have a desire to live and be known as a Christian, a desire that will hopefully grow stronger every day. But understanding the responsibility that comes with being Christian is essential, because when you bear the name of Christ, everyone taking this trip with you—everyone you meet in your day-to-day life—is likely to associate the things *you* do with the things *He* does. If you snap at a co-worker, drink illegally at a party, or put friends or homework time before your church and devotional time, people will notice. And they will think that you, and *all* Christians, don't really believe what you say they do, or, even worse, that you don't desire God more than anything else. The way that you live, the people you allow to become your intimate friends, the clothing you wear, and the habits you form are the subtlest and yet the most powerful ways to show others who owns your heart, no matter where you go or what campus you attend. Remember that your patience, respect, and love go a long way and that God will be there to work through you the minute you ask Him to.

So, are you ready for the journey?

 J.U.

Melby, Derek. "Why Students Abandon Their Faith." Center for Parent/Youth Understanding, 2008. **www.cpyu.org/Page.aspx?id=361896**

Regnerus, Mark D. and Jeremy E. Uecker. "How Corrosive Is College to Religious Faith and Practice?" SSRC, 2007. **http://religion.ssrc.org/reforum/Regnerus_Uecker.pdf**

eleven

Connecting Back Home

My friend Keisha, a freshman in college, was irate—angrier than I'd ever seen her, counting the three fights between her and her boyfriend that I'd already witnessed that semester. She had stomped into my dorm room, thrown her backpack on the floor with as much force as her petite body could muster, and now stood, shaking, hands curled into fists.

"I can't take it anymore!" she declared. "I just can't take it!"

I waited for a few cautious minutes before asking, "Can't take what, Keisha?"

"My *Mom*!" She started pacing around the room, waving her hands in the air like my crazy English professor. "She's been calling me every single day, bugging me about my classes and asking how much money I spent on the Halloween decorations and telling me about *every single thing* my step-sister's kid does, which isn't much since he's like three weeks old . . . and I just want her to LEAVE ME ALOOOONE!"

Well, of course I laughed—it was just so funny to watch Keisha rant and rave. But it was also obvious from her level of frustration that her relationship with her mother was being strained by her new status as a college student and the communication challenges that had been presented to her. Since then, I've noticed that many college students go through similar problems, in part because their ideas about connecting back home differ from those of their parents and in part because they simply don't talk about it. As you prepare for college, the small amount of planning needed to define communication boundaries can greatly reduce the potential friction that can occur between you and the family and friends you leave behind.

Springers, Clingers, and Scaling the Cliff

Connecting back home can be compared to going rock climbing with one or several partners (if you read the last chapter, you know that I love extreme sport analogies). Let's say you are smoothly scaling the side of a steep cliff, your rippled arms (hey, you've been working out, right?) pulling you easily upward as your sturdy legs support you from beneath. You're a safe cookie, so you're wearing a harness, with a rope attached to a metal anchor screwed securely into the rock face and connecting you to everyone climbing below. If you wanted to, you could pull out your pocket knife and saw through the line, breaking your tie to your partners and the potential control they have over you, but this would remove all their ability to offer you help when you need it, and it would send the message that you don't care that they are giving up their time to do this with you. Conversely, you could wrap the rope several times around your waist and twine it in figure eights through your legs, but while this would mean you were very much in touch with your partners, it wouldn't exactly give you an edge in your quest to reach the top of the cliff. In fact, it would probably keep you from doing much of anything except sliding laterally across the ledge you're currently occupying and looking . . . ah . . . ridiculous. It's obvious that in order to make progress and reach the top of the cliff, you need both the freedom to move in the direction of your choice and also the tension of those climbing with you to keep you safe.

The way students stay connected to their family and friends at home when they leave for college is a very similar phenomenon. There tends to be a fairly wide range of communication styles. On one end of this range, we have the students I call "Springers." These individuals are absolutely ecstatic to be getting out from under their parents' protective wings and into the real world. They "spring" off to their prospective universities without looking back, getting so involved with friends and activities that they practically forget they *have* a family . . . until, of course, they need gas money or a place to stay during Thanksgiving break. They essentially cut the rope between themselves and their partners (or parents).

College students at the other end of the spectrum are the "Clingers," those who would have stayed in high school indefinitely if they hadn't been handed a diploma and shoved out the door. These students call home at least once a day, visit every weekend, and are sometimes so homesick they consider ditching their dream of being a physical therapist for a career in babysitting-my-little-sister. Like a rock climber who cocoons himself in his lifeline, they wrap themselves so tightly in their former relationships that they keep themselves from creating and nurturing new ones. Most people will fall between these two extremes, of course, but any inclination toward either end can have negative effects on students' health, stress levels, and social and academic lives at college. In order to keep your connection to home strong and healthy but still allow yourself room to grow, you will need to consider how you are going to handle telephone calls, weekend visits, and your parents' access to your personal information.

The Big Idea of the Century

Before we go any farther, it is absolutely necessary I make sure you understand one vital fact of life. Ready? Okay, here it is: IT'S NOT ABOUT YOU!

I'm not kidding—it really isn't. Picture a leaf. Any leaf. This leaf probably believes (mistakenly, of course) that the sun shines solely to warm him, that the tree he lives on is there to provide him shelter, bring him water, and let him party with his friends. He probably also thinks that any work he does creating sugar or converting carbon dioxide to oxygen is part of the fulfilling life he has chosen for himself. But he's wrong. You know that, because you can see the bigger picture. You know the leaf absorbs sunlight and creates food for the tree, which is one of hundreds of trees in one of millions of forests providing shelter for animals, lumber for humans, and oxygen for everyone. And you know that, when the leaf's vibrant green hue fades to yellow or orange and he drifts slowly down to enrich the forest soil with his nutrients, the larger scheme of life will continue smoothly and indefinitely, even though the leaf has ceased to be.

You and I, though we may sometimes feel like the reason for the earth's existence, are just like the leaf. We are important (after all, the Creator of the universe designed us personally and entrusted us to do His work), but in no way do we live for other people to serve us. Connecting back home is not something we should do if and when we feel like it; neither is that connection something we should use to block out all other parts of our life. There are other people involved. Therefore, when deciding how often we should call home, we should not just let our need for parental support or homesickness motivate us but also our parents' need for information and assurance of our well-being. They don't exist for you, just as you don't exist for them. You both exist for God. In the same vein, if you are using your parents and friends at home to fulfill all your relationship needs and not becoming involved at school, you will lose the opportunity you have been given to reach out to new people and allow God to use you in their lives. As you begin the process of planning how you will react to communication and connection challenges once you begin your college semester, remember that your personal plans are only a tiny section of a much bigger one—God's.

||||||||||||||||||||||||||||

Talk About It

After all this discussion about the many ways in which communication can go wrong, you might be wondering exactly how you can keep yourself from sliding into one unhealthy extreme or the other. The trick to knowing how you will communicate later is (surprise!) communicating *now*. You can't know your parents' (or siblings' or friends') expectations about your soon-to-be-long-distance relationship until you talk to them, so do it. Sit down with your parents and ask how often they would like updates on what you are doing in school, what form of communication they would like you to use (telephone, e-mail, etc.) and how much detail they desire about your life. If you find that your parents want more time than you think you'll be able to give them, calmly tell them what you had in mind. Be prepared to compromise—if you think once-a-week phone calls are more than adequate but your mom wants to talk to you daily, try settling at three times a week and show her you are committed to being there for her by setting aside a specific block of time that you will call (for example, I talk to my mom on my way back from my last class on Tuesdays and Thursdays). You can do the same thing if your roles are reversed and your parents need very little feedback but you are extremely homesick. Explain that you don't want to be a burden, but hearing about your sister's spelling bee or how many people showed up at the church picnic really helps you to get through the day at school. Most likely, your parents will be more than happy to give you the time you are asking for.

Some of you might be frowning as you read this. *Wait a minute,* you say, *my mom is my best friend, and you're telling me it's "unhealthy" to talk to her every night?* No. I'm not. I'm telling you it *might* be unhealthy. Only you know your personal circumstances and can gauge whether you are using your relationship with those at home as a crutch. If you are uncertain whether your communication habits are damaging or not, pray about it. Ask God to show you if the time you are spending talking to your parents (or siblings or boyfriend) is taking you away from other areas of your life He wants you to be strengthened; be willing to respond to what He shows you.

‖‖‖‖‖‖‖‖‖‖‖‖‖‖‖‖‖‖‖‖‖

Homeward Bound—The Weekend Visit

Unless you are attending a distant university and don't have the finances or the necessary transportation, you will probably go home several times a semester (if you are a Clinger and find yourself going home every single weekend, see the special note below.) These weekend or holiday visits are often sources of tension. Typically, the reason for this tension stems from differences of opinion between students and parents about rules—both those that have changed and those that have not.

For example, one rule that frequently stays the same when students return is the existence of a curfew. Melanie, a psychology student from the University of Texas, found herself getting into heated arguments with her father about how late she could stay out with her friends when she came home. After managing her own time for several weeks at school, she hated the idea of anyone rearranging the schedule she'd planned out for herself. The continuance of curfews is a major stumbling block for many college students who see themselves as independent adults capable of making their own decisions.

If you identify with these students and are having trouble accepting your parents' rules, you might want to think about whether you really are independent. Are your parents in any way paying for your tuition or living expenses? How about your car or health insurance? Do you receive a monthly allowance of gas money? If any financial aid is coming your way from either of your parents, you are still technically dependent on them and should do your best to comply with their wishes.

But even being fully independent of your parents doesn't let you off the hook when it comes to following rules, because your independence means that, while their house is still your home, you are now a *guest* there. As a guest, you should be extremely considerate of your parents' desires and should take care that you are doing your part to make your visit pleasant for them as well as for yourself. This might mean cleaning up the mud you tracked in after playing that backyard football game, keeping the bathroom countertop spotless instead of scattering it with all of your hair products, washing the pizza pan you dirtied last night, and yes, coming home at eleven or twelve on a Friday even though at school you'd never dream of going to sleep until two in the morning. Once again, communication is key. Have a deliberate discussion with your parents about what they expect of you when you come home and then make a strong effort to do as they ask. If you feel their demands are unreasonable and you want to scream and throw a tantrum, don't. You'll look silly, and you won't be at all supporting your case for being an adult. Remind yourself that the Bible puts parents in a position of respect and commands us to honor them, and then suck it up and do it.

Special note for Clingers: Most likely, if you are making a beeline for home as soon as class lets out every Friday, you are keeping yourself from experiencing the opportunities offered by college life. While it is impossible for me to analyze your personal reasons for your frequent visits, it would do you a world of good to honestly evaluate your motives. If you have difficulty making friends, don't know how to find interesting activities for the weekend, or simply prefer the safety of a place where you know you will be accepted, you aren't alone. Casey, now a sophomore at a community college in Colorado, had a terrible first semester in which she struggled to meet people and get involved in activities. Because she lived only half an hour from her campus, she found herself driving home every chance she got. Eventually, her mom took her aside and suggested she spend more time at school, and so she agreed to reserve at least two weekends every month for staying on campus. "I also asked Mom to help me find something to do so that I wouldn't be so homesick," says Casey, "and she helped me go online and find a community service group that takes some pressure off single moms by doing crafts with their kids on Saturday mornings." After volunteering with this group for a few weeks, Casey had not only found an activity she enjoyed but had also made friends with two other college girls who shared her interest.

If you need help getting involved, check out your college Web site for information about clubs and activities or call your recreation center to find out if they offer fun programs such as kickboxing or water polo. An especially great place to get involved is in your church, youth group, or campus Christian group. (For help getting started in these areas, check out Chapter 10.) If you are trying to get involved but can't seem to connect with people, rearrange your mentality from struggling to fit in *yourself*, to helping someone *else* fit in. At any gathering, classroom, or church service, find someone who looks really uncomfortable and introduce yourself. You might be surprised how the person responds. And always remember that if you are willing to go where God wants you, He will give you every ounce of the strength you need to follow through.

It's My Life—The Privacy Issue

A final source of friction between parents and college students is the question of how much access parents should have to students' grades, finances, and health records. In most cases, you will be given the option to either disclose your personal information or keep it completely to yourself.

(Because of federal HIPAA [Health Insurance Portability and Accountability Act] laws, plus the fact that you are legally considered an adult starting at age eighteen, colleges are prohibited from sharing your personal information without your prior consent.)

Some students have no qualms with parental involvement (I, for one, am more than happy to let my mom see my records—she has reminded me of more than one impending deadline in the past). However, others simply prefer a greater degree of privacy. If you are one of the latter students, please keep in mind that when your parents ask if you are maintaining a decent GPA or whether you have stopped buying so many iced coffees since the last time you talked, they are not being nosy so much as they are trying to help you grow into a successful and savvy adult. This doesn't mean you have to answer every private question you are ever asked, but do try to offer at least some responses in order to put your parents at ease and show them you are cooperating.

||||||||||||||||||||||||||

Time to Climb

Hopefully, this chapter has been helpful in addressing the problems you might face when you attempt to blend your new life at college with your old one at home, but even if your unique issues were not listed here, the big ideas we discussed should apply to almost anything. Communicate. Compromise. Reach out to others. Remember that it's not about you. Pray. And get ready for one heck of a climb.

 J.U.

twelve

Safety Initiatives and Crisis Management

Have I not commanded you? Be strong and courageous. Do not be frightened, and do not be dismayed, for the LORD your God is with you wherever you go. Joshua 1:9

Individual Safety

College is wonderful fun, but interspersed with the fun is a very present danger. Rapes, robbery, and shootings happen every year, on almost every campus. While they may seem distant in relation to you, realize that it is only dumb luck that allows you to think that way—the chance that you could be next is just as likely that it will happen to someone you have never met. A personal mantra of mine has been

"Better paranoid than dead." This does not mean that I wear a tinfoil hat and carry around a bazooka. Rather, I practice constantly being aware of my surroundings and how to react in certain situations so that in the event that one occurs, I will know how to get out of it safely. There is no need for panic or a constant state of paranoia—look at it simply as a fact of the world, and learn as much as you can about that fact.

Please do not assume the mentality of "it'll never happen to me." Far too many people are killed by thinking that way. The Bible tells us repeatedly that God will protect us, and protect us He does—but even He can only do so much if you happily waltz into the den of a predator. The world is a serious place at times, and you need to practice facing it in a serious way.

||||||||||||||||||||||||||

Think Ahead

Preplanning is the key to survival. The reason more people do not do it is because it takes a lot of thought and a lot of energy. But your life is worth it!

Be aware of what could happen. Speaking from personal experience, it is advisable to go so far as to hypothesize constantly, no matter where you are. When you are walking, make note of corners that you cannot see around, or hidden nooks and crannies where someone could hide. Steer clear of them, and see what kind of hard surfaces are around that could help you in a fight. If you know your territory, you are that much more likely to survive an assault.

Rape happens. Sorry, but it does. Parties are a main place for this, so be aware of your surroundings if you happen to be a party animal. Rapes can also happen any day, any time. A sexual assault is just as likely to occur at night in a parking lot as in the middle of the afternoon in a library bathroom.

To prevent anything from happening, or to ensure that you'll be prepared when it does, plan ahead. Try to walk with a buddy as much as possible; an extra set of eyes can do wonders for the chances of spotting an assailant. It all comes down to being aware of your surroundings. If you have a bad gut feeling about someone you meet or pass on the street, act on it and stay clear of that person. Listen to your subconscious, and do not go anywhere that makes you feel uncomfortable.

Be Prepared

If you happen to run into a situation like those described above, you will need to be prepared. If your school has a light-pole system of some kind, where periodic emergency call boxes are placed, make note of them and do not be shy about using them in said emergency.

Preprogram numbers into your cell phone; the nearest campus or city police station is a good one to have, as well as the health center or hospital. Place them on speed dial, if you can, so that you can hit a button and call them while running or hiding. If your phone has GPS tracking, make sure that the system is activated and works. If you are abducted, managing to hide a cell phone/GPS tracking device on your person will prove invaluable to your rescue. The sooner the authorities know where to find you, the sooner you will be freed from your abductors, and the greater chance of your survival.

The next best method of prevention is to know people. This applies to dropping in at the fire department and making light chat with the receptionist on a slow day to paying attention to people you pass on the street. Keep your head up, and make eye contact. People who walk with their head down and their eyes on the pavement, or avoid the looks of other people, look cowed, scared, and, quite frankly, like the ideal victim. Their posture says that they will not scream and that they will be too scared to fight back. It says "antisocial" to society, and "pick me" to an assailant.

Instead of avoiding people, make an effort to know them. Smile and nod as you pass, and keep your head up. See if you can recognize people that you pass a lot, and keep their appearance in mind. Your face changes for a fraction of a second when you recognize someone, and that expression is subconsciously registered in the other person. If any assailants or would-be muggers know that you recognize them, they will be much less likely to go after you, for fear that you will be able to easily describe them to the police. And when you are not making yourself less of a target, you will likely be making many more friends. People naturally respond in a positive way to smiles.

Pay attention to the areas you find yourself in. Stick to well-lit streets and sidewalks, and keep away from the shadier parts of town and/or campus, even if it takes longer to get to your destination as a result. Look around often, and make mental notes of people that you see around you. Check behind you every few minutes—people have a tendency to rarely look above, below, or behind them, and it is from these ignored vantage points that predators often attack.

Perhaps most importantly, choose whom you hang with. If you need to go somewhere at night, grab a friend who is either very vocal (for screaming) or very observant to come with you. At parties, only leave with people you trust. This does not include the group of frat boys that you were half-drunkenly introduced to during a chugging contest. You do not know them, and you should not trust them, no matter how cool the party is that they say they will be going to afterwards, or how popular they are. Even if they are the most popular cheerleader or jock on the school football team—if you do not know them and are not friends with them, do not trust them or go anywhere with them. It may sound a bit extreme, but you will live longer because of your caution.

One of the more popularly spread stories at Florida State is of a serial killer, Ted Bundy, who preyed on the sororities around campus. He looked like a student—young, attractive, and charming. He might have passed for a model, and his manners and speech were impeccable. No one would have suspected that he would hurt a fly. His method of capture, similarly, was more refined than waving a gun around. After targeting a girl, usually alone or drunk, he would wear an arm sling or a cast, drop his books, and make sadly pathetic attempts to pick them up. When a girl bent down to help him, he would club her over the head with his cast, drag her off, rape her, and then kill her. Some of these attacks happened in broad daylight. While the facts of the case are a bit more convoluted than this condensed version, the moral of this ghost story is to implicitly trust *no one*.

Assume that every stranger you meet in the dead of night may have a gun concealed underneath his jacket, or that her purse has a brick in it. Be polite and friendly, but also be confident, maintain eye contact, and avoid exposing your back to the stranger. After passing on the street, pay close attention to any shadows you can see in front of you that may indicate close following. If you feel especially uneasy, turn around and check. It may feel awkward the first sixty times you check, but when you look around the sixty-first time and see the stranger walking back toward you with a gun or knife in his or her hand, you'll be grateful that you have that much more warning.

IIIIIIIIIIIIIIIIIIIIIIIIIII

Mugging and Theft Attempts

Parking lots are notorious for being good places for mugging. Many people will rifle through their purse or pockets for a car key and this will divert their attention from what's going on around them. Some cases are snatch-and-grab, where the mugger runs up, grabs the purse, and darts away. If the purse is on your shoulder, this means that you will likely be knocked over and your shoulder dislocated, or, in a worst-case scenario, your neck snapped from the fall or backlash. Carry your purse instead in your hands. There is nothing contained within that is worth your life or your safety.

Some cases are more direct. The mugger will approach calmly, asking for directions, an opinion, advice, or something similar. The person will often intrude on your personal space to surprise you, and then either take the purse and run or wrap his arms around your neck and choke you. Do not let anyone get close enough to do anything of the sort.

Many safety procedures will be embarrassing when they are not in serious use. Get used to this.

Screaming, especially girlish screams, squeals, or gasps, is rarely effective. Opt instead for a short, punched, loud yell from your diaphragm. Much like the "Kia!" cries used in martial arts, this will not only take your attacker off-guard, but it will be far more effective in alerting nearby people. Instead of just shouting "Kia!" though, and hoping to channel your inner Bruce Lee, shout something along the lines of "Stay back. STAY BACK!" or the ever-popular "RAPE!" Most muggers, when their prey starts bellowing at them, will abandon the idea and bolt.

For the sake of argument, though, let's assume that you have laryngitis and cannot scream or shout. Now we are into trickier territory. You will need some kind of defense training if you want to keep your purse and/or your life. Your life should be your first priority. Throw your purse as far away from yourself as you can; if it is what the mugger is after, he or she will go after the purse, leaving you free to run like mad in the opposite direction.

Mace, especially the type on small key chains, is a great deterrent. It will allow you the time to run away that you need. If you are going to carry it, though, practice with it at least once (in open air, never inside, and preferably away from other people) so that you know how to use it. Then practice putting it at the ready daily, until it becomes a habit. You can draw it five times on the mirror or on your first five attackers—your pick.

Some people prefer to carry small pocket knives, whether on a key chain or in their pocket. The mind of a college mugger can quickly be changed by seeing and feeling a defensive knife cut. Again, though: if you are going to carry it, know how to use it. Practice in open air and away from other people. Look up hand-to-hand combat books, and see what they say about knife use.

In the event that you are not keen on carrying around weapons, use whatever you have. Bug spray will work to irritate the eyes, and wasp spray in particular is effective. While it may be bulky to carry with you, having a can in your room and in your car is definitely doable. Wasp spray, a nerve agent, shoots up to thirty feet in a concentrated stream; it can cause serious and permanent nerve damage to the eyes. While drastic, this measure can make an assailant drop a knife and collapse screaming to the ground. Congratulations. You have just legally survived your way to live another day.

If it is a male attacker and he is close enough to kick in the groin, do not do so. Knee him in the groin instead. If you kick, you present the attacker with your foot, which may be caught, twisted, and used to break your leg. The knee is much closer, much harder to catch, and is akin to slamming a stone in the area.

If the attacker has you in a hold from behind, throw your head back and break his or her nose with your skull. At the same time, try to pull yourself free. Pain is a distraction—if you cause the attacker pain, you shift the focus from holding onto you to *OH ____, MY NOSE*. Use the distraction time wisely to either injure the attacker further or make your escape.

Of course, these tips alone are not enough to ensure formidable defense. Take a defense class, whether at the local YMCA or at the police station (they usually offer some kind of defense class, especially when located on college campuses, and if they do not, they will know of someone who offers a good class). Practice. Repeat the defensive move until it is in muscle memory, and then continue to practice it.

It is true that Jesus instructed us to love our neighbors. It is also true that He instructed us to turn the other cheek when injured. However, the Bible says that "if a thief is found breaking in and is struck so that he dies, there shall be no bloodguilt for him" (Exodus 22:2). As God's children, we are not supposed to take the law into our own hands unnecessarily or strike out in anger, but neither are we instructed to sit idly during a theft or attack. If your life, or the life of someone you care about, is in danger, *you must act.*

You cannot afford to be shy or halfhearted in your defense. Your goal is to hurt the attacker badly enough that you can get away. If that means snapping an arm to get the person to drop a weapon, then so be it. You must be willing to do what it takes to protect yourself and your friends. Once you are mentally ready for that, the rest will come into play.

The "Always" Rules

There is a certain set of behavior that you should endeavor to follow regardless of the time of day, where you are, or what you just finished eating. By following these guidelines, you can significantly reduce your risk of being singled out for an attack.

Only a surprisingly small number of people walk actively. The word *actively* here means "with conscious attention to one's surroundings." Take a look at the people you pass on the way to your next class. How many of them are looking at the ground, reading a book, talking on a cell phone, texting, or listening to music? All of these things are distractions, and they do not improve your level of safety.

Looking at the ground is a subconscious act that says, "I am too shy to interact with others. My mind is not focusing on anything in particular right now." This is the red flag that attackers look for. Keep your head level and your actions alert, and maintain a constant, if casual, scan of your surroundings.

If you absolutely must talk on a cell phone or text while walking, especially through a parking lot or at night, maintain an active scan of your surroundings, and keep your conversation short. Do not rummage in your purse or backpack for something as you talk, as your brain is now divided between three activities (walking, talking, and searching) and will likely not register the shadowy figure off to your right.

Wanting to listen to music as you walk is understandable, but it is antisocial behavior (you have effectively tuned other people out) and will make it harder to hear shouts or gunshots. It is also a distraction, as part of your brain is concentrating on the words of the artist and not the words of those around you. Save the tunes for studying in your room, and enjoy the air and conversation while you walk.

Another underused tool is the buddy system. You learned it in elementary school, and somewhere along the path to college, you have dropped it under the assumption that it is now "childish" and therefore not for your use.

WRONG. Wrong, wrong, wrong.

The buddy system is invaluable. You have a companion to talk to, an extra set of eyes to help you keep watch, and an extra voice (probably with an extra cell phone) to call for help if you should need it. Try to avoid going anywhere alone at night. It is a recipe for robbery, and walking along a poorly lit road by yourself at midnight or one in the morning is not the smartest action you could take. Most college security systems offer a free escort if you just call to make the request. You may have to wait for a few minutes, though, so plan for that and stay in a well-lit area until the escort arrives.

The beautiful thing about college is that there is almost always someone going your same direction. It may be a kid from class, or someone from your youth group. It may be someone whose name you forgot from the dorm introduction social. Whomever you choose to walk with, make sure that you at least choose *someone*.

As stated before, think proactively. Be aware of your surroundings, and think like a robber yourself. Where would be a good place to hide? Are you small enough to be taken down by one person, or big enough that you'll face two? Where is a well-lit area that you could run to? Where is the nearest telephone or open office building?

The sooner you start planning for an attack, the better prepared you will be to face it should one present itself.

||||||||||||||||||||||||||||

Campus Crisis

With the exception of a shooting, what was described previously in this chapter was largely an address of personal risks that you may encounter. There is an entire extra category of safety hazard that you may face, and it will be severe enough to affect more people than just yourself.

Weather

Weather is a part of nature. Bad weather happens, and chances are good that it will happen several times over. A hard fact to learn is that you are not more powerful than natural forces. A tornado will not stop when you set foot out the door, and a hurricane will not vanish because a paper is due.

Never risk your safety against the weather. If a tornado warning is in effect, and you know that that means to stay inside, then you need to stay inside. Teachers *will* understand that you were being cautious, and most of them allow you to skip three or four classes without penalty for this precise purpose. The weather is not so forgiving or lenient.

In the event that natural forces threaten, follow the school procedures set in place for this kind of occurrence. Of course, this means that you need to read and familiarize yourself with the school procedures. Know where to go in case of a fire, and where the highest ground is if you are at risk in a flood. Find out where you are supposed to meet if a tornado sweeps through campus, and in the event of a power outage, keep extra batteries and a radio on hand.

Listen to weather forecasts, whether on television or on the Internet. Pay attention to them. In the event of a lightning storm, respect the danger that can come from a trillion-volt lightning bolt and batten down with some popcorn, friends, and a board game.

Shootings and Lockdowns

In March 2007, thirty-two students on the campus of Virginia Tech were killed by a single gunman. Less than a year later, six students were killed and eighteen wounded on the campus of Northern Illinois University. (See "Dealing with Crisis on Campus" at the end of this chapter.)

Shootings can happen anywhere, anytime, and without any warning. Almost always, someone ends up dead. To ensure that you are not included in the body count, familiarize yourself with the school's policy for shootings. If there is a phone number to call to report a shooting or a very upset someone waving around a gun, preprogram that number into your phone, or write it on a piece of paper and keep it inside your wallet. Get a map of the campus and spend your early weeks familiarizing yourself with the larger buildings. Then, in the event of such an emergency, you will then be able to ascertain where the danger is in relation to you and maneuver accordingly.

Make sure that you always have a way to communicate. If you are like the 90 percent of college students who own a cell phone, keep it on your person in class. Even if your phone is on silent, keep it powered on. If you have to call emergency services, you will need to dial quickly, and you may not be able to afford the ten seconds it takes for the phone to power up.

In the event of a shooting, keep low to the ground and try to get behind some kind of cover. Concrete or metal is preferable, but anywhere out of eyesight of the shooter is better than standing around screaming. If you hear a shot and see a gun, drop to the ground, then and there. It is much more difficult to shoot something on the ground, as there is more of a distortion of depth perception and much less area to be hit.

Many schools offer the option to sign up for e-mail and text alerts. You should take advantage of this offer. If you are in a class or in your dorm room, the text or e-mail may be the only way for you to find out about the danger present on campus. Stay informed, and you will stay safe.

Epidemics

Remember how easily colds were passed around in high school, especially if it was crowded? Triple that risk, and you will have a good idea of what disease on a college campus is like. It may not always be as innocuous as a head cold, either. Viruses are easily passed around, as are bacteria, and there are some that will make you terribly sick, if not kill you. Keep in mind that students at your college are not all from your country—they can come from anywhere around the world, and with them may come travel-loving bacteria and organisms.

Make sure you have had all required immunizations by the time you first set foot on campus. These vaccines will reduce the risk of you contracting a disease and will help you fight it off if you manage to pick it up anyway.

Wash your hands and sanitize regularly. All sorts of people from all venues of life have touched the desk where you are sitting, and while a mild amount of contamination is actually good for your immune system, there is no need to be stupid about it. Wash your hands after you use the toilet and before you go to eat. Bring hand sanitizer along in your book bag, so that if you happen to get into something gross through the day (think boogers or gum stuck to the underside of a chair or desk as best-case scenarios), you can quickly clean your hands and go.

Avoid sharing anything that has had contact with bodily fluids of any kind, even lip gloss. College students will "make out" and more on a regular basis. It's been a part of the campus experience for many, many years, and it will not change any time in the near future. Even if you trust your friend, you cannot trust your friend's boyfriend or girlfriend, and if you accidentally share spit with your friend, you are partaking in the spit of that boyfriend, girlfriend, and anyone else that third person may have hooked up with at a party.

The good news is that by eating properly and taking vitamins as needed, you will probably be just fine. Taking care of your body's dietary needs fulfills a huge part of staying healthy and disease-free. By making sure you have enough to draw from, you are more likely to bounce quickly back from a cold or flu virus.

In the event that whatever disease you have picked up does not go away, or becomes more serious than you thought, kick your pride aside and go to the health center. That is, after all, what it is for, and the sooner you go get the proper antibiotics for whatever bug it is that you've picked up, the more quickly you can be firing on all cylinders and not having to pay fees for classes you cannot attend.

Enjoy Life!

"For God gave us a spirit not of fear but of power and love and self-control" (2 Timothy 1:7).

I realize that this last chapter may not have been as rosy as the prior eleven. Do not dwell on it. Death is a part of life; you could die as easily from a shooting as you can from a major car accident. Somewhere in your childhood, you were hopefully told that a hot stove can hurt but, if used properly, it can feed you and help you to live. Similarly, that is what I have tried to express in this chapter, only on a more adult level. Everything has the potential to injure—it is how you perceive it that makes the difference.

Life is meant to be lived. Use your common sense, and you will be just fine. Ask for help when you need it, and help others when you can. Love and treat others as you would yourself. For more assurances in dealing with campus crisis, keep reading to see how God works in spite of tragedy. Pastor Marty Marks shares his personal perspective following the shootings at Northern Illinois University.

 L.F.

Dealing with Crisis on Campus— A Personal Story

Whenever you hear first responders to a crisis speak about what they did and how they were able to perform their duties while "under fire," they almost inevitably say something to the effect of "This is what we train for!"

When a gunman opened fire in a crowded lecture hall on the campus of Northern Illinois University on February 14, 2008, I bolted out of my office and across the field to the campus, where I was met by a rush of bloody and terrified students running the opposite direction. They were literally running for their lives! What prepared me and many others to deal with this crisis both in the immediate aftermath and in the days and weeks that followed? Well, this is what we train for!

God trains us in our daily walk with him to trust Him. Day in and day out, He sees us through all of life's struggles. Some are more stressful than others, but at the end of the day, God uses our daily walk to shape and form us to serve Him better and better. Our time in His Word, in worship, in and partaking of the Sacraments are all part of that "training." When a crisis like the one on my campus happened, those years of being trained to care for others more than myself, the earnest desire to show compassion like Christ did, and a sense of urgency about His mission pretty much compelled me to rush in where His presence was needed. He had already overcome death on the cross; what really was there to fear?

How did I know what to say or what to do? Well, honestly, I didn't really think about it. I did what I always do; I turned to God for help and support and encouraged others to do the same. I encouraged others to stay calm and to look for ways to care for those who were hurting, even in the midst of their own anxiety.

The Valentine's Day celebrations that had been planned for that day stood in stark contrast to the terror and bloodshed that resulted from the shooting spree. I specifically remember speaking to a Community Adviser (a "CA", also known as a Resident Assistant or "RA" at other universities) about the big Valentine's Day party that had been planned for that evening. Those many plans now needed to be scrapped. Though the party was cancelled, the CA very quickly organized some students to bake cupcakes that would have otherwise been used for the party and take them door-to-door, handing them out to anyone who needed some "cheering up." This took place within only about an hour or two of the shooting. Ten days later, when NIU resumed classes, that same CA celebrated Valentine's Day with the party that was originally planned, saying, "The shooting can't take this away from us." I *loved* her spirit! Tragedy may shake us, but it can in no way take from us what is promised to us.

That same "spirit" should be ours. Nothing can take from us what God has promised—to always love us and care for us; and in that caring He has promised to use us as His presence. During the days afterward, I often quoted the 2007 movie "Evan Almighty," where the God character says, "*Let me ask you something. If someone prays for patience, do you think God gives them patience? Or does He give them the opportunity to be patient? If they pray for courage, does God give them courage, or does he give them opportunities to be courageous? If someone prayed for their family to be closer, do you think God zaps them with warm, fuzzy feelings, or does He give them opportunities to love each other?*"

I asked the same of the people on our campus. As people prayed for peace and comfort and unity for our campus, I simply asked, "Do we think God will zap that into our campus, or is He giving us the opportunity to *be* His peace, comfort, and unity on our campus?" From there, the rest was easy; I needed to be a calm, loving presence like Jesus, offering His love to all who would listen, and sometimes sharing His love simply with a hug. Let's face it. This is what we train for in our walk with God every day!

 *M.M.*